Eyewitness Accounts of the American Revolution

Narrative of the Death of Major André

Joshua Hett Smith

The New York Times & Arno Press

MAJOR ANDRÈ

The Portrait engraved by Hopwood, from a drawing by Major Andrè. The Ornament by Shirt.

AN

AUTHENTIC NARRATIVE

OF THE CAUSES

WHICH LED TO THE DEATH OF

MAJOR ANDRÈ,

ADJUTANT-GENERAL

OF HIS

MAJESTY'S FORCES IN NORTH AMERICA.

———◆———

BY

JOSHUA HETT SMITH, ESQ.

COUNSELLOR AT LAW, LATE MEMBER OF THE CONVENTION

OF THE STATE OF NEW YORK.

———◆———

To which is added

A MONODY

ON THE DEATH OF MAJOR ANDRÈ.

BY MISS SEWARD.

═══════════

London:

PRINTED FOR MATHEWS AND LEIGH, 18, STRAND.

1808.

Printed by W. Clowes, Northumberland Court, Strand.

ADVERTISEMENT.

THE author of the following sheets feels it incumbent upon him to observe, that he has no ambition to appear as a man of letters; he has only a simple narrative to relate, which will promote the sacred cause of truth, and exempt him from the frequent interrogations of his European and Trans-Atlantic friends. The object of this work is to elucidate a transaction, the most important that occurred during the progress of the American war.

The fate of the author was so much blended with that of Major Andre, that he considers it necessary to connect them together; as it will tend the more effectually to explain many circumstances which would otherwise appear very obscure.

In consequence of his agency in this interesting affair, his own life was placed in imminent danger; and the pens of the historian and the traveller have been unjustly and illiberally exercised on the subject. Although their ignorance and partiality are eminently conspicuous, the author conceives it a duty which he owes to his own character, to expose their fallacies; particularly, as there is no person who possesses the means of explaining this subject more fully than himself.

The business being of a political nature, on which much has been said, written, and conjectured, he is well aware that many of his readers will be more or less influenced by their former opinions; coinciding with, or dissenting from his statement, agreeably

to their former prejudices. From these,
however, he solicits a candid retrospect of
their sentiments; while others, to whom the
subject is novel, he hopes, will derive satisfaction from his reflections on many of
the causes that produced the event in question—an event, which occasioned the death
of an amiable and gallant officer in the
most ignominious and tragical manner—an
event, that has occasioned more misery to
the author, than the pangs of death.

In the following pages the writer will
make no other comments than those naturally arising from the facts that will be
stated, and proved. Hence there will be
no grounds for the exercise of malignant
cavil, or partial criticism; and the inquirer
after truth will be better able to draw his
own inferences, and judge how far the narrative is worthy of credit.

The author feels it his duty to apologise for any unbecoming appearance of egotism; for, as he was a party in the tragical drama, personification, in detailing it, becomes unavoidable: yet he cannot but lament the painful task thus imposed on him, of vindicating his own reputation against the illiberal attack of the Marquis de Chastelleux, (a general in the French service, under the command of Count Rochambeau,) in his work stiled " *Travels through North America, in the Years* 1781, 1782, *and* 1783;" and also in another publication, recently and accidentally placed in the hands of the narrator, and from whence he has taken the extract with which the narrative commences.

After a perusal of this volume, the candid reader will judge how far the insidious writer of the extract, just mentioned, from the " *Political Magazine for February*, 1781," has been influenced by truth or liberality;—the author will only generally remark that, from beginning to end, it is a base fabrication; and that, in those days of heat, jealousy, and party, when men's minds were mutually inflamed —when the standard of Discord waved triumphant, and friend and relative armed in her cause, the licentiousness of the press was carried to an unwarrantable height, and no rank, or character, however elevated, was free from the venom of slander.

NARRATIVE

OF

THE CAUSES WHICH LED

TO THE

DEATH OF MAJOR ANDRE.

———

Extract from the Political Magazine for February, 1781.
" CIRCUMSTANCES RESPECTING THE BETRAYING OF MAJOR
ANDRE.

" WHEN Major Andre went to consult
with General Arnold, he was carried to the
house of a Mr. Smith, brother to the Smith,
lately appointed Chief Justice of New York,
by General Robertson, and also brother to a
Dr. Smith, who lately lived in Downing-
street, Westminster, and who is said to have
gone off the morning that the soldiers fired

B

on the rioters, and whose negro woman was
hanged for being concerned in the burnings.
While Major Andre was communicating
with General Arnold, he lived at the house
of Smith, and wore Smith's clothes, and
when he set out from Washington's camp,
Smith attended him till within about twelve
miles of Knightsbridge, where Andre told
him he knew his way perfectly well. Just
after Smith left him, he was taken, and, at
that very time, he had on Smith's clothes.
Washington has tried Smith for being concerned in what they call Arnold's conspiracy; but the trial has turned out a mere
farce; for Smith has not suffered any punishment. The people at New York therefore
believe, that Smith betrayed Andre to the
rebels, and are of opinion that he never can
clear up his character any where but at the
gallows."

THE gloom and melancholy in which my unhappy agency had involved me, as just described and misrepresented, rendered it necessary for me to travel; and to adopt all rational means to obliterate the remembrance of the miseries I had endured:— hence I carefully secluded myself from those associations that might have a tendency to renew my affliction of mind; and it is from this cause that I have so long been ignorant of the calumnies propagated by the artful, the interested, and the designing, to injure my character; while the public have hitherto been precluded from obtaining a representation of facts.

Before entering upon the narrative that forms the subject of the following pages, it will be necessary to observe, that in the time of the American War, a free communication between Canada and New York, by means of the Lake Champlain and Hudson's Ri-

ver, was of the utmost importance, in
order to facilitate the operations of the British
arms in the meditated plan of subjugating
the Colonies; it was equally the interest of
America, from every principle of sound
policy, to counteract this measure. A
chain of mountains extending along the
banks of this river upwards of twenty miles,
between Stony Point and Slaughter's Landing, near New Windsor, prevented a regular ferry from being established, to preserve the communication between the
eastern and southern states, for the con-
veyance of supplies of provisions, and for
the marching and counter-marching of the
troops of the confederacy. It therefore
became necessary that a fort should be
erected for the above purpose, to check any
naval force that might obstruct the passage
of the boats employed at the ferries.

For this purpose Fort Montgomery was

erected in 1776, and a strong boom laid
across the river, guarded by two frigates;
the Hudson being navigable for ships of
war of 60 guns much higher than this fort,
and, at spring tides, for frigates near to Albany. In 1777 Fort Montgomery was attacked and carried by Sir Henry Clinton,
who passed it in his attempt to favour the
descent of General Burgoyne from Canada,
in the autumn of that year, and in all probability a junction of these armies would have
been effected, had the expedition been earlier
adopted, as meditated by Sir Henry Clinton.
The interception of a courier happened at
that time in a manner so singular as to be
worthy of attention; and to describe which
I shall make a short digression.

The courier dispatched by General Burgoyne to General Sir Henry Clinton, was
charged to deliver to him a silver bullet, and
to give it into the General's own hands. In

case of surprise, if challenged from whence
he came, or suspected of being an enemy,
he was ordered to swallow the bullet, which
would prevent the message from being de-
tected.   Having reached as far as Fort Montgomery, near New York,* he made enquiry
for General Clinton; and finding, on being
brought before him, that he was not the person described to him as the General to whom
he was sent, but that he was GOVERNOR-
GENERAL GEORGE CLINTON OF THE
STATE OF NEW YORK; he turned aside
and swallowed the silver ball.   Being observed by some of the attendants, he was immediately taken into custody; when being
interrogated as to what business he had with
General Clinton, and discovering some em-
barrassment in his answers, it was proposed
to administer an emetic, to ascertain what he
had swallowed with such precipitation.   The

* When this transaction occurred, the narrator resided in the vicinity.

idea was adopted, and the consequence was,
that he threw up the silver ball ; which being
unscrewed, was found to contain a letter
from General Burgoyne to General SIR HEN-
RY CLINTON, the purport of which was to
explain his forlorn situation, after the attack
of General Arnold at the heights of Bremen.
The courier was immediately hung as a spy.

Upon the reduction of Fort Montgomery,
the royal force proceeded up the Hudson, to
the vicinity of Albany, carrying fire and devastation before them.   On both sides of the
river the shores were undefended by mountains, opening to an extensive champaign-
country, well inhabited by substantial far-
mers, of whom two thirds were unfriendly to
the dismemberment of the empire by the
measure of independence of Great Britain.

The town of Kingston, beautifully situated near the west bank of the Hudson river,

was laid in ashes by General Vaughan; it had been the seat of government. The convention of the State of New York had here formed their new constitution, and it was likewise here that Rose and Middagh, two leaders of the loyalists in that part of the county of Ulster, were executed, without a regular form of trial, for their adherence to the royal cause; this circumstance, with others of a similar nature, had rendered the place extremely obnoxious to the loyal followers of the British arms, and possibly might have occasioned its conflagration. A large body of loyalists were forming at this time on the eastern shore of the river to join the royal army, but the advanced state of the season prevented the continuance of the British force in the river, and they were compelled to disperse on the advance of the American troops, on the surrender of General Burgoyne in 1777.

The name given to this place by the first Dutch settlers was Esopus : it is now called Kingston, and is celebrated in Chief Justice Smith's History of the province of New York, for affording the best flour and draft horses on the Continent of America, as well as a particular beer, in great request for its nutritious qualities.

If the importance of obstructing the navigation of the Hudson existed merely in idea, previous to this event, the erecting of an insurmountable barrier against the British navy became now indispensably necessary. Commissioners were therefore appointed to examine the passes of the high lands, and a point of land projecting in the river on the west side, not far distant from Fort Montgomery, called West Point, was selected, from the natural advantages presented, for this purpose ; not only from the strength of the

circumjacent ground, but from the narrow-
ness of the Hudson, which here takes a short
winding circuit east and west, uniformly
different from its usual course of north and
south.   This defile was fortified by a strong
boom thrown across the river, and a range of
fortifications ascending to the highest mount,
a natural platform, on which was erected the
strongest work, called Fort Putnam; this
was bomb-proof and unassailable, from its
strength and elevated situation, being built
on and composed of rocks, of which the
place abounded.   As this post was not to
be flanked, it was of course deemed impregnable; in the confidence arising from which,
it was abundantly stored with every military
means of defence that the country was capable of affording at that stage of the war, and
made the grand arsenal of the main army.
The communication above the garrison being
thus secured, it was capable of being sup-

plied by water carriage with all weighty articles, essentially requisite as well for defence
as to render it a general magazine.

This important pass was commanded in
the earlier part of the campaign of 1779 by
Major-General Howe, one of the oldest officers in rank in the American service; he
was a particular favourite of General Washington. General Howe had been previously
in the British service; was well versed in
tactics, a rigid disciplinarian, and was acknowledged to be an engineer of the highest
reputation. He had had the command of
Fort Johnson at Cape Fear, in North Carolina. Possessing these qualifications, and
his zeal in the service being evident, he was
high in the confidence of General Washington. General Howe, upon assuming the
command, contributed by military art to that
invincible defence formed by nature to render West Point impregnable. Eighteen

miles below West Point were erected the
two forts of Verplank and Stony Point, (the
first on the east, the last on the west side
of the Hudson river); at the entrance of
this range of mountain, a ferry had long
before been in use, called King's Ferry, and
which was protected now by these forts,
which were esteemed the dependencies of
West Point, and considered as *the key of
the American Continent.*

General Howe being desirous of a more
active command in the line of the main
army, immediately under the direction of
General Washington, the latter conferred
the important trust of West Point to General Arnold, who, being lame from the wounds
received in the several actions in which he
had gallantly shared, from the walls of Quebec
to the plains of Saratoga, was thought from
those circumstances, and his approved bravery, most worthy of succeeding General Howe.

The prowess and gallantry of General Arnold, evidenced in his rapid rise from the
rank of a captain to a major-general, in the
short space of three years, while it proved
his merit, justified Washington's appointment, for which he received the sanction of
Congress, and the applause of the people.

The invincible spirit which he and his
hardy followers encountered in their march
through an inhospitable desert is inconceiv-
able. They proceeded from the camp at
Cambridge to Quebec, subjected to cold,
hunger, and fatigue, (far surpassing in difficulty and distress the march of Hannibal
across the Alps,) reduced almost to starva-
vation, and, however incredible it may seem,
compelled occasionally to eat the leather of
their shoes and boots !

During this distress, every man in his
army recollected the general's patient and

indefatigable zeal at the siege of Quebec,
where he received a wound; his prudent
and well-conducted retreat through Canada,
and gallant defence of the American fleet on
Lake Champlain; the whole of his career in
the reduction of the army under General
Burgoyne, whose defeat was principally
ascribed to Arnold's singular bravery, and
his attack of the royal troops in Connecticut under General Tryon, against a far superior force; all these circumstances had
raised his reputation to the highest eclat
among his fellow-citizens, and insured him
the most perfect confidence in the army and
in Congress.

Although his conduct at first drew
upon him the resentment of the executive
council of Pennsylvania, when in the command of Philadelphia, and for awhile eclipsed
his rising glory, yet a judicious court-martial, after the most strict and impartial inves-

tigation, acquitted him of every charge that could in the least impeach his integrity; and General Washington, in confirmation of their decision, conferred on him the command of West Point as a mark of special favour and distinguished approbation, and earnestly pressed his assuming the command against New York, on the junction of the allied army under Count Rochambeau.

At this period he visited my house with his family, on his way to his appointment. I opened my doors with hospitality for his reception, as I had done generally to the officers of the army, and other genteel travellers, being always ready to shew such attentions, from the amplitude of the means I then possessed. I spread my table with cheerfulness for his entertainment, and conceived his acquaintance as an honourable acquisition. Little did I then conceive I was dispensing hospitality to a man whose defection from the cause he had so gallantly maintained afterwards astonished the whole world.

My house was situated on the nearest route, where all communications generally passed from the eastern and southern states across the ferry at Stony Point, about 18 miles below West Point. General Arnold's residence, while commanding the garrison, was at the house and farm of Colonel Beverly Robinson, who had relinquished them, and joined the royal army at New York. This residence was situated opposite to West Point, on the eastern side of the Hudson, a dreary situation, environed with mountains, and no way calculated for the residence of a lady of Mrs. Arnold's taste, she being well qualified, from a most amiable disposition, and every engaging attraction, to be at once the example and ornament of the politest circles. Being at that time but recently returned from Charleston, South Carolina,

with my family, Mrs. Smith was equally destitute of the society which each had been
accustomed to in their respective cities.
The intercourse by land or water from West
Point to Stony Point in the summer season was easily attained ; they were therefore
engaged in frequent visits to each other, and
General Arnold was as frequently with me,
in search of those culinary supplies, unat-
tainable in his mountainous recesses. I felt
myself happy in rendering him every aid in
my power, and cultivated his acquaintance
from motives of security; for in my absence
from the State of New York, my family in
general were suspected of disaffection to the
American cause ; my eldest brother, the late
Chief Justice of Canada, having been banished within the British lines at New York
for his unequivocal attachment to the English government ; another brother, who was
generally deemed an enemy to the revolution,
and myself, were also more than suspected

C

of being in the British interest, from the circumstance of my being appointed, with two
other gentlemen of the county of Orange, a
Doctor Butwater and Colonel Sherrard, (by
a very large majority of the electors of that
county) to oppose in the convention of de-
legates of the different counties of the province in 1776, the measure of Independence
then recommended and adopted by Congress. Indeed, such was the jealousy of the
times, that to be descended immediately
from English parentage, or to possess any
lukewarmness in the rash and intemperate
measures that the demagogues of the mob
chose to dictate, was sufficient to render the
tenure of life, liberty, and propery, most precarious.

From the elevated situation I possessed,
commanding an extensive view of the capacious Bay of Haverstraw, at this part of the
river five miles wide, I frequently observed

flags of truce passing and repassing*; and I took the liberty of requesting to know from General Arnold if there was any impropriety in the simple interrogation, whether the flags were for an exchange of prisoners by cartel? He answered generally, that in a short time the business of the flags would be explained. Soon afterwards, it was mentioned at dinner by General Arnold, that the flags had brought letters from Colonel Beverly Robinson, who, General Arnold said, was very anxious to make terms for the recovery of his estates, that had been confiscated to the public use; and that Colonel Robinson was authorized to propose, through his medium, some preliminary grounds for an accommodation between Great Britain and America. Colonel Lamb of the Artillery, at West Point, an old and sagacious officer, who, with a number of other officers from the garrison, was present at dinner, immedi-

* This was early in September, 1780.

ately said, that any proposition of that kind
ought with more propriety to be made to
Congress, than to a General, only commanding a district; General Arnold replied,
that the communication must at first be
made through some channel, and here the
conversation ended.

Some time afterwards General Arnold, in
another visit, seemed more communicative;
he expressed his detestation of the *French
alliance*, from the perfidiousness of their national character; ridiculed the solecism and
inconsistency of an absolute monarch being
the ally of a people contending for freedom,
who kept his own subjects in the most des-
potic and absolute slavery; thought it was
an unnatural union, of no duration, and that
it was not made by France until she saw the
Americans were able to defend themselves,
which would be more to their own national
honour and glory. General Arnold then

mentioned that he had received another flag
of truce, and that Colonel Beverly Robinson
had anxiously solicited an interview, to be
more explanatory of the propositions that
were to produce, if acceded to by Congress,
a general peace, and happily terminate the
expence of blood and treasure, that were
ruinous to both countries, in the prosecution
of a war without an object.   He said he
conceived that the overtures made on the
part of Great Britain by her commissioners,
the Earl of Carlisle, Governor Johnson, and
Mr. Eden, (now Lord Auckland) were
founded in ALL SINCERITY and GOOD
FAITH, that they fully met the *ultimatum*
that the generality of the Americans desired,
but by what he could learn from Colonel
Robinson, the present terms held out went
much farther than the propositions of 1778,
and he made no doubt that they would be
the basis of an honourable peace; this event,
he said, he most cordially wished, being

heartily tired of the war; and he then complained of being ill used by Congress and the
executive council of Pennsilvania, which *had
treated him with injustice*, in not *sufficiently*
ESTIMATING HIS SERVICES*.

I requested to know from General Arnold
if he had informed General Washington of
Colonel Robinson's applications, and what
was the General's opinion of the business?
He answered, that he had written to him for
directions how to act, but that he was then
gone to Connecticut or Rhode Island, on a
visit to COUNT ROCHAMBEAU, the commander in chief of the French troops, lately ar-

---

   * At the time of this interview, General Arnold
was at my house; and, in the familiarity of conversation, he expressed himself as follows:—" Smith,
here am I now, after having fought the battles of my
country, and find myself with a ruined constitution,
and this limb (holding up his wounded leg) now rendered useless to me. At the termination of this war,
where can I seek for compensation for such damages
as I have sustained ?

rived from France. Soon after this conversation, I accompanied my family on a visit to
Fish Kill, a settlement about 18 miles higher
up the river from Robinson's house, where
I left them; and stopping at General Arnold's quarters on my return, agreeably to
his particular request, he solicited me to
conduct a flag of truce to the VULTURE
sloop of war, then lying in Haverstraw Bay,
for the purpose of bringing Colonel Beverly
Robinson to the intended interview.   I was
so deeply interested in the object of this meeting, as represented to me by General Arnold,
and the success of it was so congenial to my
wishes, that I made no hesitation to assure
him of my cheerful concurrence; and in a
day or two afterwards, *General Arnold came
to my house at Haverstraw with the necessary
passports for my mission to the Vulture.*

Having *himself* made the necessary arrangements, such as providing a boat from

the quarter-master, Major Keirs, at Stony
Point, with every publicity, I was surprised
that he should request me to go in the night.
He begged of me to procure for him hands
from among my tenants *that had been used
to the water.* I stated to him the impropriety
of conducting a flag in a manner which I
deemed unprecedented; but he overruled
my objection by assurances that it was properly *understood on board the* Vulture,
and that the business was of a nature not to
be generally known for the present among
the citizens. Having made the promise, I
could not recede, and with much reluctance
I consented to go; but he had great difficulty to persuade my tenants to accompany
me, as they were intimidated by the danger
of the undertaking by night, nor would they
have consented, although *promised* handsome
pay, and menaced with confinement for their
non-compliance, if I had not appeared willing to countenance the measure, assuring

them it was, in my opinion, for the good of
the country, which, upon the representations
of General Arnold, were my real sentiments.

Accordingly, after General Arnold had
given the order for muffling the oars, that we
might not be impeded by the boats that
guarded the shores, a precaution necessary,
as there was a regular water patrole, to prevent those disaffected to the American interest, or Tories, as the friends to the royal
cause were called, from carrying provisions
or intelligence to the British ships occasionally lying in the river.   This precaution,
however, staggered the confidence of the
eldest of the watermen, who bluntly told
General Arnold that if the business was of a
fair and upright nature, as he assured them
it was, he saw no necessity for any disguise,
or to seize the veil of night to execute that
which might be as well transacted in broad
day-light.   The watermen were simple, ho-

nest men, had been accustomed to their oc-
cupation, and were my tenants, in whom I
could place the utmost confidence; and it
afterwards appeared I was not deceived.
General Arnold insisted on their pursuing
the business, and assured them he had the
command of the militia of the country for 60
*miles round West Point by order of Congress,
and that he would give a countersign to the
guard boats, that we might pass unmolested.*
The countersign given was CONGRESS; thus
arranged, no farther hesitation was made to
gain the VULTURE, then lying at the extremity of Haverstraw Bay. The night was
serene, the tide favourable, and the the silent
manner in which we passed the fort at Stony Point, at the mouth of Haverstraw
Creek, precluded any obstructions; in short,
although the distance was nearly 12 miles,
we soon reached the ship. On our approach
we were hailed by the centinel on deck, ordered to bring to, and questioned whither

bound? I answered, with a flag of truce to the *Vulture sloop of war*, upon which I was heartily assailed with a volley of oaths, all in the peculiarity of sea language, by the Officer commanding the watch on the quarter deck, and commanded instantly to haul alongside, or he would blow us out of the water. Upon coming alongside, I was saluted with another discharge of the same nautical eloquence; and orders were given to hoist the rebel rascal on board, which was prevented by my climbing up a rope fastened to the main chains, and so reaching the main deck. I was questioned as to my business, and how I could presume to come on board his Majesty's ship under colour of a flag of truce at night? To which I answered, I was so authorized by my papers, which I requested he would give to Captain Sutherland, the commander of the ship, and Colonel Robinson, as I knew they were on board; this request, however, seemed to have no effect;

but he poured on me torrents of abuse,
threatening to hang me at the yard-arm, as,
he said, another rebel had been a few days
before; being nevertheless unintimidated,
and seeing Colonel Robinson and the Captain, for whom I had letters, I raised my
voice and said, he must be answerable for
my being delayed: whether I was heard in
the cabin or not I cannot say, but soon afterwards a boy came on deck and said, " *the
captain orders the man below*;" he conducted me into the cabin, where on my entrance I saw a venerable looking gentleman,
whom I recognised to be Colonel Beverly
Robinson, dressed in a regimental uniform.
He received me politely, desired me to be
seated, and shortly introduced me to Captain Sutherland, who lay ill in his birth.
Colonel Beverly Robinson having perused
the letter from General Arnold, apologized
for retiring a few minutes, ordering some refreshment, and left me to converse with

Captain Sutherland, to whom I related my uncourtly reception on deck; and his amiable urbanity compensated me for the incivility of his officer on deck. Having conversed with Captain Sutherland for twenty minutes on indifferent subjects, Colonel Robinson returned, and introduced Mr. Anderson to me, saying he was mentioned in General Arnold's letter, for whom he had sent a pass to come on shore, in case he Colonel Robinson should be unable to accompany me. Colonel Robinson pleaded indisposition, and said Mr. Anderson could as effectually answer all the purposes by going on shore as himself; there seemed no reluctance on the part of Anderson to supply Colonel Robinson's place, and he appeared in a dress equipped for the purpose, wearing boots and a large blue great-coat. For my own part it made no difference to me who bore me company, so that the object of my mission was fully answered, and the great national ends obtained, which Arnold assured me would be the result of the affair.

Mr. Anderson being ready, we left the ship, and were rowed in a short time to the western shore, to the place which General Arnold had appointed for the interview; this was at the foot of a mountain called the Long Clove, near the low water mark, whither my servant had conducted General Arnold, on horseback, he being still lame from his wounds.

Very little conversation passed between Mr. Anderson and myself, excepting trivial remarks about the tide, the weather, and matters of no concern. Mr. Anderson, from his youthful appearance and the softness of his manners, did not seem to me to be qualified for a business of such moment; his nature seemed fraught with the milk of human kindness.

On my approach to the place of appointment, I found General Arnold ready to receive me; he was *hid among firs.* I mentioned to him Colonel Beverly Robinson's reason for not accompanying me, and the delegation of a young gentleman, a Mr. Anderson, whom I had brought with me, and who was then with the watermen on the strand. He appeared much agitated, and expressed chagrin at the disappointment of not seeing Colonel Robinson. He desired me, however, to conduct Mr. Anderson to him, which being done, he requested me to remain with the hands at the boat. I went as directed, but felt greatly mortified at not being present at the interview, to which I conceived myself entitled from my rank in life, and the trouble I had taken to effect the meeting. At length they continued such a time in conference, that I deemed it expedient to inform them of the approaching dawn of day. Shortly afterwards both came

down to the boat, and General Arnold, with
much earnestness, solicited me to return
with Mr. Anderson to the Vulture; but I
pointed out the impracticability of effecting
his wish, from the great distance, and the
fatigue of the hands. He then applied to the
men, who declared themselves unable to gratify his wish, through want of strength to accomplish it, and the ebb tide being against
them. Convinced of the apparent impracticability of the attempt to reach the ship, and
return before day without being discovered
from either shore by the inhabitants, whose
eyes were constantly watching the move-
ments on the river, not only from the forts,
but the surrounding shores, he relinquished
his solicitations, and desired I would endeavour to return the boat to the place from
whence we first embarked: this, with much
labour, and taking the circuit of the eddies,
was nearly effected, (as we left the boat at
Crane's Island) when our attention was

called to the cannonade from Gallows Point against the Vulture, which was compelled to fall down the river, and appeared to be set on fire; Colonel Livingston, however, must have been totally unacquainted with General Arnold's designs, or he never would have fired at that time upon the ship.

I will here again request the candid and liberal reader to judge whether any man in his senses would or would not have refused to carry Mr. Anderson back to the Vulture, if he knew the extent of General Arnold's plot, and the danger to which he was exposed in case of a discovery. If the purport of the interview had been fully accomplished, why could not General Arnold have given me a flag, to carry this gentleman on board the Vulture? The fact is, he had not recovered the trepidation into which he was thrown on Mr. Anderson's first landing, from what cause let the reader form his own opinion. Julius Cæsar did not discover more intrepidity than General Arnold, who, in the many actions in which he was engaged, never retired without some scar or wound, as honourable testimonies of bravery.

On my return home, I found that General Arnold and Mr. Anderson had arrived long before, Mr. Anderson having mounted the horse my servant had rode, when he followed General Arnold to the Long Clove, the place of Anderson's landing. He appeared vexed that the ship had been compelled to leave her position; and, after taking breakfast, and my ague coming on, it being the day of its return, I was obliged to retire, as well on that account as to recover from the fatigues of the night; so that General Arnold and Mr. Anderson were left alone the far greater part of the day. The conversation at breakfast was principally about the arrival of the fleet at New York, under the command of Admiral Arbuthnot, the general health and spirit of the British army, and other desultory topics of no consequence. Towards the evening Arnold came to my house, and proposed that I should convey Mr. Anderson back to the Vulture, which had nearly regained her former situation; he saw, however, from the state of sickness under which I then laboured, with a fit of the ague upon me, that I was unable to gratify him; on which he proposed my accompanying him part of his way on his return to New York, by land, as soon as my health would permit, on the removal of the ague fit; to which I made no objection, as, when better, it would be in my way to visit and bring my family home from Fish Kill, being obliged to cross the river for that purpose. He soon after returned, and told me a difficulty had occurred, of which he was not before apprised; for that Anderson had come

on shore in a military dress, which he had
borrowed, from pride or vanity, from an Officer of his acquaintance at New York; that
as it would be impossible for him to travel in
that uniform, he requested the loan of one
of my coats. Being nearly of my size, I lent
him a coat: the other part of his dress, he
said, did not require change. General Arnold then proposed returning to his command at West Point, leaving Mr. Anderson
very disconsolate with me. I endeavoured
to amuse him by shewing him the prospect
from the upper part of my house, from
whence there was an extensive view over
the capacious bay of Haverstraw, to the opposite shore; he cast an anxious look towards the Vulture, and with a heavy sigh
wished he was on board. I endeavoured to
console him by the hope of his being at the
White Plains, or New York, before her.
Finding myself better, I promised to accompany him on his way. I could not help

remarking to him, that I thought the General might have ordered a flag of truce from
Stony Point, to have returned him to the
Vulture, without the fatigue of his going to
the White Plains, that appearing to me a
circuitous route, unless he had business to
transact at that place of a public nature.
From this time he seemed shy, and desirous
to avoid much conversation ; he continued
to urge preparations for his departure, and
carefully avoided being seen by persons that
came to the house.

Previous to his quitting it, General Arnold had prepared a passport for him to go
to the White Plains, and a flag of truce for
me to go thither and return. Finding myself better, and refreshed with the rest I had
taken, I ordered my servant to get the horses
in readiness, and we reached the ferry at
Stony Point before it was dark, intending,
if the weather should be fine, to proceed as

far as Major De la Van's that night, at a place called Crum Pond, the distance of about eight or ten miles from the ferry, where I knew we should be well entertained, and take the dawn of the morning to proceed with more satisfaction. Between my house and the fort at Stony Point, our conversation was principally about the taking and re-taking of that place; I found my fellow-traveller very backward in giving any opinion, or saying much about it. We were met on the road by several officers belonging to this post, with whom we conversed very freely, and stopped at the sutler's at the ferry to drink with them. When we arrived on the opposite side, we rode up to the tent of Colonel Livingston, the commanding Officer at Verplanks Point; I being well acquainted with him, he having served his clerkship and studied the law with my brother, the late Chief Justice of Canada, and being also a relation of Mrs, Smith; he pressed

us to stay to supper with him, but this Mr.
Anderson seemed desirous to decline. As we
proceeded, I thought he grew more cheerful, and as our road became better, we rode
on with an increased speed, and had reached
about five or six miles when we were challenged by a patrole party. On advancing,
the commanding officer, a Captain Bull,
demanded a countersign before we should
pass, and drew his corps about us; he
enquired who we were, the reason of
our travelling in the night, and from whence
we came? I told him who I was, and that
we had passports from General Arnold, the
commanding officer at West Point, which
we had received from the general that day;
that we were on the public service, on business of the highest import, and that he
would be answerable for our detention one
moment; he insisted on seeing the passports,
and conducted us to a house in the vicinity
where there was a light: on approaching the

house Mr. Anderson seemed very uneasy;
but I cheered him by saying our papers would
carry us to any part of the country to which
they were directed, and that no person dare
presume to detain us. When we came to the
light I presented the passports, which satisfied the captain; but he seemed better pleased
when I told him I intended to quarter that
night at Major De la Van's who, he said,
was a staunch friend to the cause of his
country, would treat us well, and render
every aid in his power that tended to promote the welfare of America; he soon began
to be more pleased, and in the most impressive manner intreated us not to proceed one
inch farther in the night, as it was very dangerous, for the Cow Boys had been out the
preceding night, and had done much mischief,
by carrying off cattle, and some of the inhabitants as prisoners. Alarmed at this intelligence, I was hesitating what to do, when
my companion expressed his wish to pro-

ceed; but the captain suggested many pru-
dential reasons why he would not advise our
progress at night.   He particularly re-
marked that we had little chance of defend-
ing ourselves against both parties then out,
as he had heard them firing some little time
before he met us.   All this determined me
to take the captain's advice, which seemed
to direct the surest step for our safety.   I
accordingly returned a short distance, to look
for night-quarters, and my companion reluctantly followed.

Cow Boys was a name given to those who
were in the British interest; while the name
of *Skinners* was the appellation of their op-
ponents; the latter were a banditti, who in-
discriminately plundered friend or foe; and
all those who were peaceable people and
had property, were subjected to their con-
tributions: a good horse, a fat ox, a cow,
or a pig, were the particular incentives for

plunder, outrage, inhuman barbarity, and
even murder. This was the unhappy state
of a district more than fifty-five miles in extent, in one of the oldest and best settled
counties in the government, where, literally,
brother was against brother, and father against
son, frequently imbruing their hands in each
other's blood. All friendly intercourse was
at an end, for each was jealous of the other,
and no one slept safely in his bed. Many
families hid themselvels at night in barns,
wheat-ricks, corn-cribs, and stacks of hay;
and, on each returning day, blessed their
good fortune that their houses had escaped
the flames. Knowing these facts, from living so near the spot, and frequently seeing
the unfortunate sufferers that fled from it, I
was very thankful for Captain Bull's advice
not to risk the ride by night, and cheerfully
consented to adopt it.

With no small difficulty we therefore re-

turned several miles, and gained admittance
into a house for the night; while such was
the caution and danger of admitting noctur-
nal inmates, that we were obliged to take to
bed or keep the family up, who would not
retire until they saw us safely lodged. We
slept in the same bed; and I was often disturbed with the restless motions, and uneasi-
ness of mind exhibited by my bed-fellow,
who on observing the first approach of day,
summoned my servant to prepare the horses
for our departure. He appeared in the
morning as if he had not slept an hour during
the night; he at first was much dejected,
but a pleasing change took place in his countenance when summoned to mount his
horse. The landlord, who was a very kind
and civil man, (I think his name was M'Koy)
refused to take any compensation for the
trouble which we had given him. He, too,
had been plundered of nearly all his horses
and cattle. He therefore most devoutly

supplicated vengeance against the authors
of the war, and wished himself back to
the Highlands of Scotland. I stopped at
his house on my return. M'Koy's blunt-
ness pleased my companion; he professed
himself a loyal adherent to the crown. It
was singular that the Scotch in the southern
states were attached to the royal interest,
but to the northward their principles were
diametrically the reverse, some few instances
excepted: but to whatever party they adhered, they discovered the national character
of invincible integrity to their trust.

We rode very cheerfully towards Pine's
bridge without interruption, or any event
that excited apprehension; here I proposed
to leave my companion; but I observed
that the nearer we approached the bridge,
the more his countenance brightened into a
cheerful serenity, and he became very affa-
ble; in short, I now found him highly enter-

taining; he was not only well informed in
general history, but well acquainted with
that of America, particularly New York,
which he termed the residuary legatee of the
British government, (for it took all the remaining lands not granted to the proprietary
and chartered provinces.)   He had consulted
the Muses as well as Mars, for he conversed
freely on the belles lettres: music, painting,
and poetry, seemed to be his delight.   He
displayed a judicious taste in the choice of
the authors he had read, possessed great elegance of sentiment, and a most pleasing
manner of conveying his ideas, by adopting
the flowery colouring of poetical imagery.
He lamented the causes which gave birth to
and continued the war, and said if there was
a correspondent temper on the part of the
Americans, with the prevailing spirit of the
British ministry, peace was an event not far
distant; he intimated that measures were
then in agitation for the accomplishment of

that desirable object, before France could
establish her perfidious designs, He sincerely wished the fate of the war could alone
be determined in the fair, open, field-contest,
between as many British in number as those
under the command of Count Rochambeau
at Rhode Island, whose effective force he
seemed clearly to understand ; he descanted
on the richness of the scenery around us,
and particularly admired, from every eminence, the grandeur of the Highland mountains, bathing their lofty summits in the
clouds from their seeming watery base at
the north extremity of Haverstraw Bay.
The pleasantry of converse, and mildness
of the weather, so insensibly beguiled the
time, that we at length found ourselves at
the bridge before I thought we had got half
the way ; and I now had reason to think
my fellow-traveller a different person from
the character I had at first formed of him.

This bridge crosses Croton river, a branch
of the Hudson; here we halted, and at a
low house on the right endeavoured to obtain some breakfast, from an old matronly
Dutch woman, and provender for the horses;
in this expectation, however, we were disappointed; the Cow Boys or Skinners had
been there the night before, and taken all
the supplies of her cupboard, except some
Indian meal, which she had mixed up with
water, and boiled into a consistency, by the
Dutch called *suppon*. This, with the addition of some milk, from a single cow they
had mercifully left her, was the only fare we
could procure, and it being remarkably
clean, (for which the Dutch of the country
are deservedly celebrated) we made a good
meal; our appetites being keen from having
been supperless the preceding night:---While
at breakfast I mentioned my determination
to proceed no farther. Having discharged
the bill to the woman, in the local money of

the county, my companion requested me to
lend him some, and I cheerfully supplied him
with the half of my pocket amount, although I
was afraid it was not current below that
place; the bridge being accounted the south
boundary of the American lines. He was affected at parting, and offered me a valuable
gold watch in remembrance of him, as a
keep-sake, which I refused. The horse was
furnished by General Arnold; the saddle
and bridle were borrowed of me, with the
promise that they should be returned, or the
value of them paid to me.

Having given him directions about the
road he was to take upon crossing the bridge,
with a message to my brother, the chief
justice, whom he knew, we parted. I proceeded on my way to Fish Kill, taking General Arnold's quarters at Robinson's house
in my route: I mentioned to General Arnold the distance I accompanied Mr. Ander-

son, which gave him apparently much satisfaction.   His dinner being ready I partook
of it, refreshed my horses, and in the evening proceeded to Fish Kill to my family.
Here I found General Washington had arrived in the course of the afternoon, on his
return from visiting Count Rochambeau,
and I supped in his company, with a large
retinue, at General Scott's.   The next day
I went on business to Ploughkeepsie, and returned to Fish Kill the ensuing evening.   It
was on the 25th of September, about
midnight, that the door of the room
wherein I lay in bed with Mrs. Smith,
was forced open with great violence,
and instantly the chamber was filled with
soldiers, who approached the bed with
fixed bayonets.   I was then, without ceremony, drawn out of bed by a French officer,
named Govion, whom I recollected to have
entertained at my house not long before, in
the suite of the Marquis de la Fayette.   He

E

commanded me instantly to dress myself,
and to accompany him to General Washington, having an order from the general, he
said, to arrest me. The house was the residence of Colonel Hay, who had married
my sister. The family was thrown into
great confusion; the female part especially
were in the deepest distress; indeed, the
shock so much affected Mrs. Smith, that
she never fully recovered from it; and, which
added to my subsequent sufferings, was the
cause of her death. I perceived that any
opposition would be ineffectual; Colonel
Hay desired to know for what cause the
arrest was made? to which Govion would
give no satisfactory answer. I then desired
the privilege of having my servant and one
of my horses to go with him to General
Washington, at Robinson's house, which
he refused; and I was immediately marched
off, on foot, the distance of eighteen miles.
At length on my arrival at Robinson's house,

I was paraded before the front door, under a guard. General Washington soon afterwards came into a piazza, and looked sternly and with much indignation at me; my countetenance was the index of my mind, and the beautiful lines of Horace occurred to me, " *Si fractus et illabiter orbis impavidum feriuntque ruinæ,*" &c. On his retiring, I was ordered into a back room, and two centinels placed at the door.

After as much time had elapsed as I supposed was thought necessary to give me rest from my march, I was conducted into a room, where were standing General Washington in the centre, and on each side General Knox and the Marquis de la Fayette, with Washington's two aids-de-camp, Colonels Harrison and Hamilton.

Provoked at the usage I received, I

addressed General Washington, and demanded to know for what cause I was brought
before him in so ignominious a manner?
—The general answered sternly, that I
stood before him charged with the blackest
treason against the citizens of the United
States; that he was authorized, from the
evidence in his possession, and from the
authority vested in him by Congress, to
hang me immediately as a traitor, and that
nothing could save me but a candid
confession who in the army, or among
the citizens at large, were my accomplices in the horrid and nefarious designs I had meditated, for the last ten days
past.

I answered, that no part of my conduct
could justify the charge, as General Arnold,
if present, would prove; that what I had
done of a public nature was by the direction

of that general, and, if wrong, he was amenable ; not me, for acting agreeably to his orders.

He immediately replied, " Sir, do you know that Arnold has fled, and that Mr. Anderson, whom you have piloted through our lines, proves to be Major John Andre, the Adjutant-General of the British army, now our prisoner ? I expect him here, under a guard of 100 horse, to meet his fate as a spy, and, unless you confess who were your accomplices, I shall suspend you *both* on yonder tree," pointing to a tree before the door.—He then ordered the guards to take me away.

In a short time I was remanded into the room, and urged to a confession of accomplices, with General Washington's declaration, that the evidence he possessed of my being a party, was sufficient to take away my life.

I answered, that as a citizen I did not conceive myself amenable to a military jurisdiction; that I well recollected when he came forward from Philadelphia to take the command of the army at the camp at Cambridge, the provincial congress of New York addressed him for the purpose of preserving the rights of citizenship; his reply to them was, that " when he assumed the character of the soldier, he did not forget that of the citizen; and that he looked forward with pleasure to that auspicious period, when the rights of his country being secured, he might retire to the sweets of peaceful tranquillity under the protection of the law." I told him I could not conceive that any simple recommendatory resolve of Congress, to which he alluded, could abrogate a fun-

damental clause in the constitution of the
state, of which I was a member, and which
had, for the benefit of the subject, established the right of *trial by jury* in all cases
whatever; that it was a violation of that
right, which congress had assigned, amongst
others, for their separation from Great Britain, and which had given birth to the present war.

Enraged with the force of this reasoning,
with vehement indignation he ordered the
guards to re-confine me.

Some time afterwards, Colonel Hamilton
came to me, and compassionately, as he
said, recommended me to declare all I knew
respecting the business of which I was accused, observing that many were mistrusted,
who, if they confessed, would be in a worse
situation; but as he supposed this was not
my case I had now a chance to save my

life, and for the sake of my family I ought
to preserve it, with many more expressions
to the same effect, &c.

General Washington then came into the
room, and in the most imperative tone questioned Colonel Hamilton why he was so
long speaking to me? The colonel replied,
" General, I know Smith has meant well
during his agency in this transaction, for in
all our public meetings at New York his
general demeanour spoke a spirit of moderation, nor could he be persuaded to any other
opinion than that this contest between Great
Britain and her colonies would be compro-
mised, as in the business of the stamp and
other acts of which we complained to the
British government, in our petition by Governor Penn; his object and the principles
of his family have been uniformly intent to
reconcile the sons of Great Britain to their
brethren in America, and in all social meet-

ings his language was, " *United we flourish,
divided we fall.*" I must therefore declare
my mind in saying that he ought to be
discharged."

General Washington then looked sternly
around, and said in a gentle tone of voice,
" Colonel Hamilton, I am not yet satisfied ;
take him into the back room ; we must
know something more about this business."
I was then conducted into the recess from
whence I had been brought ; and I entered it
greatly agitated by the extraordinary usage
I had met with.

I was about to take some refreshment,
when one of the centinels, posted at the
door, vowed that if I touched any of the
biscuits that were in the room, he would
shoot me dead. The fact was, that the
room was a kind of butlery, in which Mrs.
Arnold had placed her stores, and I was in

the act of taking a piece of the biscuit, not
having had any sustenance from 12 o'clock
the preceding day. I therefore began,
among other reflections, to think Mr. Washington, or some of the family, or suite,
might have some tenderness to the rights of
nature, in the discharge of those offices
which it requires; especially, as both at
New York and Belmont (the name of my
residence) the laws of hospitality were well
attended to on the part of my family and
myself towards General Washington. I
was particularly intimate with the general's
son-in-law Colonel Custos, when he was at
King's College, New York, for his education, a foundation liberally patronized by
his present Majesty, whose gracious benevolence was so handsomely attested by Sir
James Jay, in his narrative of his mission
to England, to collect donations towards the
support of that infant institution for the
cultivation of science. He made his voyage

in the year 1764, the discharge of which
duty is faithfully detailed by Sir James in
his reply to Barlow Trecoticke, then alder-
man of London. Sir James is a brother of
John Jay, who was the first American ambassador sent to the court of Spain, a gentleman of brilliant abilities, descended from
a French family, who left France upon the
revocation of the edict of Nantz, in the
reign of Louis the Fourteenth, for their adherence to the protestant religion. He was
one of the framers of the constitution of the
state of New York, and was, with Doctor
Franklin, at Paris, highly instrumental, as
an American ambassador, · in forming the
French alliance with America. Mr. Jay
entertained a bitter enmity against priests of
all descriptions, and at length obtained his
desire to have it ordained, as a fundamental
principle in that constitution, that all priests,
of whatever denomination, having the care
of souls, should be excluded from all secu-

lar or temporal power whatever; and to guard against all influence that the catholics might have in society, any in the communion of the church of Rome, whether as emigrants coming into that state, or otherwise, should, before they held offices of trust, renounce the influence of all princes, powers, and potentates, by oath of abjuration.

This gentleman was educated at King's College, so named in compliment to his present Majesty; he has since been in England as ambassador; he signed the commercial treaty, by the special direction of Congress, in President Jefferson's administration; and on his return to New York he was, by the mercantile influence, elected governor of that' state, the people knowing his attachment to the first principles of American opposition to the claims of Great Britain, to bind them by Lord Chatham's bill, called the Declaratòry Act, " *in all cases whatever."*   This Mr. John Jay was a son-in-law of William Livingston, the governor of New Jersey, and author of the elegant poem called " Philosophic Solitude;" was one of the committee of Congress who, with Colonel Livingston, drew up the address to the people of Great Britain, declaring their reasons for the revolt of America from Great Britain, in addition to the Suffolk resolves, as they are termed, preparatory to the declaration of independence adopted by the United States in the year 1776.

This commercial treaty not suiting the French party, after Mr. Jay's triennial government expired, agreeably to the period limited by the constitution, he was removed from the seat of Government, on that account, by the demagogues of the people, and superseded by Governor George Clinton.   Mr. Jay, disgusted with this treatment,

has been heard to exclaim, as General
Washington did, " A REPUBLICAN IS AN
UNGRATEFUL GOVERNMENT." Buonaparte
thought so too, and hence all Europe are
living witnesses, that tyranny, whenever it
is let loose, will make gigantic strides.

I made no reply to the centinel; but remained nearly two hours in this confinement, when I heard the tramp of a number
of horses near the place where I was confined, and, soon after, could clearly distinguish the voice of the unfortunate Andre,
and of General Washington and his suite,
who soothed him with all the blandishments
that his education and distinguished rank
demanded; he was courted with a smile in
the face, when worse than a dagger was intended for his heart. I distinctly heard Colonel Hamilton say to a brother officer, who
came out of the same room, that Major
Andre was really an accomplished young

man, and he was sorry for him, for the general was determined to hang him. This
expression affected me deeply, and reminded
me of General Washington's declaration,
that before the setting sun, on the arrival of
Major Andre, both of us should be suspended " on yonder tree." The justice of
the measure, or the power of putting the
threat into execution, did not for a moment
give me any concern for my own personal
safety. I knew he was enraged, nor had my
replies to his questions been in any manner
calculated to appease his anger.

The sun was nearly down, and I listened
attentively to hear my fate announced;
but all business seemed to be conducted
in whispers. In the course of my examination by General Washington, in answer to his question, " Whether I had
any written correspondence with General
Arnold ? I had answered in the affirmative,

and that his letters to me would prove the
nature of my agency with him ; and I gave
directions where to find the key of my desk,
and the drawer where Major Andre's coat
was deposited. Colonel Duer, of whom I
shall speak hereafter, was a man in Washington's confidence, and was entrusted to attend
to the search of my papers. Nothing could
be done until Duer's return ; it was late in
the day when he went, and he could not go
and return, the distance of forty miles, in
the space of time limited for my existence.
I therefore reposed myself in confidence that
I should have one night to collect my scat-
tered thoughts ; and I resigned myself to the
protection of Divine Providence.

It was nearly dark, when a very respectable young gentleman entered the room, and
politely desired me to accompany him. I
was in hopes this was a prelude to my
emancipation, and I requested the honour

of his name? he answered, " it is Washington ;" I said, " I presume, Sir, you hold
the rank of colonel ?" He told me he held no
rank at all; he then conducted me to the
back part of Robinson's house, where there
were two horses; desired me to mount
one of them, and by his guidance, in a way
I had never been, we soon reached the bank
of the river opposite to West Point. Here
I was delivered to the custody of a Captain
Sheppard, of the New Jersey Continental
Troops, and did not observe I had been
guarded by a troop of horse until I was
placed in the ferry boat, and saw them follow Mr. Washington up the mountain; two
boats followed us, composed of the guard.
If I had had any inclination to throw myself
overboard, I was so well guarded, that I am
certain I should have been taken out of the
water; for the main object of General Washington in detaining and trying me, was to
obtain the knowledge of General Arnold's
confederates in the army, as well as in Con-

gress. In fact, this defection of Arnold
had excited such a general suspicion, that
no one dare trust another; and nothing
but execrations were heard from hut to
hut.

I landed on the West Point side of the river,
and was conducted to a hut called the provost guard-room, where I was delivered to
the custody of an officer, whose name I do
not recollect. It was now dark, and I was
placed in a room in the hut without any
light, and left to choose the softest *board* I
could find for a bed. I now endeavoured to
compose my mind, and attempted to sleep,
when I was interrupted by the provost-
martial, who entered with a pair of hand-
cuffs; he was accompanied by the Reverend
John Mason, of the Scotch seceders' con-
gregation at New York. The officer was
proceeding to place these delicate ruffles on
my wrists, but was prevented by Mr. Mason, who offered to become my surety; and

I pledged my honour that I would not endeavour to effect my escape, nor accept the
assistance of others for such a purpose.
Whether this prelude of terror was intended
to intimidate me, I cannot pretend to say;
it however led me to suppose that very serious measures were meditated against my life.
The reverend gentleman, after commise-
rating my unhappy situation, and expressing
his extreme sorrow to find a branch of a
family that he so highly respected, placed
in so dangerous a predicament, assured me
that his utmost exertions should not be
wanting to alleviate the miseries of my confinement, and that if I would candidly declare to him how I came to be in such a situation, his utmost endeavours should be
made with the commander in chief to procure my enlargement. He professed to have
considerable interest with General Washington, and said that he was sent by him to
interrogate me on the subject, and that if I

would confess who were General Arnold's
accomplices, he would intercede for my
parole, to enable me to return to my family
under a guard. The soothing and consolatory conduct and conversation of this venerable gentleman would have induced me to
comply with his solicitation, had I known
Arnold's plot, but there was not a creature
whom I could suspect to be in his confidence except Colonel William Duer, whom
I saw at his house at Philadelphia in the autumn of 1778, when on my journey to
Charlestown, South Carolina; and respecting whom I had heard Arnold speak in terms
of the highest commendation.

I mentioned to Mr. Mason the substance
of what I had declared to General Washington, and he answered that the general was
much concerned to detain as a prisoner a person for whom he had a high esteem, and
from whom he had received marks of distin-

guished civility and hospitality; that the
commander in chief was the more enraged at
the defection of General Arnold than he
could have been at the treasonable conduct
of any general officer under his command,
from the uncommonly spirited exertions he
had made in the cause of his country; and
therefore he was led to suspect all around
him: that from some of his papers left behind, he appeared to have been engaged in
secret peculations with the commissioners,
as well as with the low suttlers of the garrison; and one, whom the commander in
chief strongly suspected, had absconded.
He also mentioned a letter of my own among
his papers, soliciting the restitution of a large
quantity of Indian corn, and wished to
know upon what principle I made the demand, and whether I had at any time commercial dealings or contracts with General
Arnold? I gave him the strongest assurances to the contrary, adding, that I merely

applied for a return of that quantity of corn
and forage that was forcibly seized by the
commissaries to supply the extreme exigen-
cies of the army, then upon the point of
disbanding, for want of provisions. They
had taken from the tenants of my family
estate, and other poor inhabitants, all the
means of subsistence possessed by their families, and had given them certificates for the
amount of such seizures, but for which, when
presented to the commissary or paymaster-
general, they had refused payment; stating,
that if they were to pay the losses, the paper
money of the continent would not be of the
least service to them, the depreciation then
being at seventy paper dollars for one of silver, while congress had made the standard
at forty. These poor people, therefore, applied to me to advise some remedy, and I
applied to Major-General Robert Howe, then
commanding West Point, explaining the peculiar hardship attending the situation of

these distressed families. The general, as a man of humanity, sympathized with them, and desired me to collect their certificates, make up the amount, and when the magazines at West Point were filled, which he expected would be soon, part, or the whole, of what was seized, should be restored, agreeably to the quantum specified in their respective certificates. General Howe's removal from the command at West Point, and General Arnold being appointed his successor, were therefore the circumstances that induced me to renew my application to him on this subject. The distress of the inhabitants was actually so great, that in order to obtain bread for their families, they were compelled to barter their cattle, and whatever property they could collect, as no other means remained to keep them from starvation: this state of misery induced many families to remove to a distance into the country, and suffer their farms to lay waste. They were,

In consequence, charged with being disaffected to the American cause, and upon the least suspicion that they repined at their hard lot, they were dragged before a board of committee-men, generally composed of the most violent Whigs of the country, and speculators upon the distresses of their fellow-citizens; and upon the evidence of some who were interested in the spoil, they were condemned as Tories, and adherents to the British interest. On these grounds, their names were entered into a book called the black-roll, and upon any subsequent assessment to raise money for taxes, bounties for soldiers, or other public demand, not having the means to discharge the quota assessed, they were, by warrant from a justice, distrained of whatever property they possessed, to satisfy the rapacious demand; and, in many instances, they were left naked, with their children, in the deepest state of misery.

But to return from this digression, I gave my reverend visitor all the satisfaction he could obtain from me, with many thanks for his consolatory advice. He promised, on his departure, to send me some provisions, and a blanket to rest on, an article which had not been furnished me, and he cheered me by declaring, that if what I had stated to him in my transactions with General Arnold was founded on truth, he could not conceive my case to be desperate. He then observed, there was no knowing, from the irritation of the public mind, what might be said against me; advised me to speak little, and cautiously, to any person who might ask me questions; and, above all, he concluded by telling me to place my trust in the Almighty, who had promised to be with them who called upon him in trouble. He then left me, saying that he should see General Washington, and inform me of the result the ensuing day; but I never saw nor

heard from him afterwards, nor was either
blanket or refreshment sent to me that
night.

To some it may seem extraordinary that
a clergyman should be commissioned to undertake such a business; but when I mention that Colonel Hamilton knew my partiality towards that truly good old man, they
will not be surprised; for if I had any propositions to make as a condition for my own
safety, he might most naturally suppose, if
I would commit myself at all, it would be to
a man of Mr. Mason's amiable character.
He is now no more; but he has left a son,
who is also a clergyman, and a shining ornament in his profession.

It was not uncommon in America for the
clergy to dabble in politics; as well in the
pulpit, as on all public occasions. To this
they were piously directed by congressional

resolves, authorising them to pursue such
conduct; and in some instances they were
appointed commissaries and quarter-masters.
Of one, in particular, I cannot forbear relating the following circumstance: he was
the reverend quarter-master Caldwell, and
resided at Connecticut farms, near Elizabeth
town, New Jersey. This reverend gentleman
was a most furious persecuting demagogue,
and had taken an active part in support of
the American cause on all occasions, which
rendered him an object of the keenest resentment among the persecuted persons; the
consequence was, that in June 1780, when
the royal army invaded New Jersey, under
the command of Generals Knyphausen and
Robertson, in passing by the reverend quarter-master's house, they saw his wife at the
window, and some of the new-levied soldiers instantly shot her dead. The story is
related by some with shocking circumstances
of aggravation; but it is generally believed

she had come to the window from a curiosity
to see the soldiers pass; and it was surmised
by others, that she had imprudently been
the aggressor, by hissing them, or some
other act of impropriety unbecoming her
sex. The reverend quarter-master himself
was some time afterwards shot, for intermed-
dling with matters foreign to his functions.

After Mr. Mason left me I passed the
night in the most solicitous anxiety for the
state of my family, whose distressed situation I described when first arrested by Colonel Govion. In the morning, the commissioners of sequestration at Fish Kill, the
place where my family resided, and from
whence I was carried, without hesitation
seized my phæton, horses, and black men-
servants, as well as a nephew, who inter-
posed to effect their rescue, and who was ap-
prehended and sent also under guard to West
Point, as an accomplice; but upon exami-

nation before General Washington he was
discharged, and, by the advice of counsel,
the property was returned; while my wife,
and a sister, with three young children, were
banished from Fish Kill, and on the road
home to Belmont were denied entrance at
the inns, and loaded with the bitterest execrations by the inhabitants as they passed;
in short, all who were in any way connected
with me, felt the effects of the popular prejudice.

On the morning after I was carried to
West Point, I was visited by many from
idle curiosity, and interrogated by questions
as impertinent as they were cruel. I remained in this situation until the morning
of the third day, with a scanty allowance
of provisions, and no other beverage than
water, although I offered to pay whatever
the guard would require, for any accommodation which I might receive.

I was at length paraded before the hut
and desired to march, with a strong guard,
down to the landing. When I arrived, I
saw the amiable Andre near me, amongst a
crowd of officers. On stretching my hand
out, and preparing to address him, I was
told by Major Talmadge, sternly, that no
conversation must take place between us.
Soon after this two barges, well manned,
rowed up to the landing-place: I thought
we were to proceed together, but was soon
convinced of my mistake, and was led to
the sternmost vehicle, while the tide favour-
ing, we were not long before we reached
Stony Point.

A detachment of Colonel Sheldon's corps
of horse, commanded by Talmadge, met us
here, and was part of the same that brought
Major Andre to Robinson's house : we were
soon mounted ; I was here placed in the
van, and Major Andre in the rear. Stony

Point was about two miles and a half distant from my residence. I was, therefore, anxious to see the state and situation of my property; and, on making the request, my wish was indulged. The devastation that had taken place distressed me much, but more particularly when I found that papers had been taken from a private drawer in my desk, the key of which I had given, by General Washington's direction, to the man in his confidence, Colonel Duer, whom I have already mentioned, in order to convey to the general the letters that had passed between General Arnold and myself.

In this private drawer was the value of 30,000 dollars in Loan-Office certificates, which were afterwards allowed by Congress in payment, at the rate of thirty in the pound, New York currency, the par of exchange four shillings and six-pence sterling. Finding the letters gone, which I wished to obtain

for my security, I was not at a loss to conjecture what had become of them. I found,
however, when I demanded those letters on
my trial, that they were not produced; the
person who took them was probably in hopes
of my speedy execution; and, in that case,
he would have remained unquestioned about
them. I asked Colonel Duer, some time
afterwards, for information respecting the
money and letters, when he assured me
that he saw no papers of the description
alluded to. The world, however, has not
mentioned his name with extreme delicacy;
and he certainly prevented my friends from
saving much property which was afterwards
lost.

I was re-mounted again by the officer who
attended me, and soon re-joined the troop
which had gone forward with Major Andre.

We crossed the brook which the Marquis

de Chastelleux speaks of, when the horrors possessed him on passing the house of Smith, where the liberties of America were bought and sold. " I cannot help remarking," says he, " on making this observation, that Smith is now confined against justice." How rashly do some people judge by the current tale. Being a Frenchman, he was totally unacquainted with the spirit of the great Alfred, who, in ordaining the right of trial by jury, established the principle, that every man is presumed innocent until he is proved guilty.

At the distance of ten miles, we were allowed to halt, and dine at the house of Mr. John Coe.

Major Talmadge, who commanded, here displayed uncommon kindness. After securing Major Andre with vigilant videts, I had the honour of his company, and

received many respectful attentions from
him.

After dinner we proceeded, by a circuitous route, to Tappan, or Orange Town,
and arrived there about dusk. We were paraded before the church; many of my *quon-
dam* friends flocked round me, and from
them I received the bitterest invectives.
After the arrangements were made by Washington, Major Andre was comfortably lodged
in a house belonging to Mr. Mabee of that
village, and every attention was paid him,
suitable to his rank and character. For my
own part I was ordered into the church, and
refreshment was sent me from Washington's
table. Judge Heron, of that place, an old
family friend, furnished me with a blanket
to lie on, and a provost guard was placed at
the church door, while two centinels kept
watch within the church, to prevent my
escape, with strict orders to see after me

closely.   Under all this parade of terror, as
many would have thought it, I felt myself
in calm tranquillity, and a gleam of consolation glowed through my heart, from a perfect conviction of having done no more than
my duty.

It will not be amiss here to turn back to
General Arnold, and to account for the capture of Major Andre.   I left the latter at
Pine's bridge, and had pointed out to him
the road to the White Plains, whither his
passport enabled him to go, or lower if he
thought proper, he being on public business, as was mentioned in his pass; but he
thought the road by the way of Dobbs' ferry,
having the river as his guide, would be much
the nearest route, and, having a good horse,
he boldly ventured to take that road; but he
had not proceeded more than six miles, when
he was stopped by three of the New York
militia, John Paulding, David Williams,

and Isaac Van Vert,   who, with others,
were on a scouting party, between the out-
posts of the two armies. These men stopped
Major Andre at a place near Tarry Town,
and seized his horse by the bridle in a narrow
part of the road.   Andre, instead of immediately producing his pass, asked where they
belonged to? They answered, " *to below.*"
Not suspecting deception, he replied, " *So
do I*," AND DECLARING HIMSELF A BRI-
.TISH OFFICER, INTREATED THAT HE
MIGHT NOT BE DETAINED, being on pressing business! The law of the state gave to
the captors of any British subject, all his
property, and, of course, his horse, saddle,
and bridle, were in the first instance a temptation to stop him on the least ground for
suspicion, while, he being alone, they were
the more bold against an *unarmed* man.
Finding himself thus taken by surprise, and
detained, he offered a very valuable gold
watch, which, I have before observed, he

had begged me to accept, thinking it would
induce them to let him pass ; but this led to
farther suspicion; upon which they took
him aside in the bushes and searched him,
until they found his papers lodged in his
boots ; another circumstance of suspicion
was the coat I had lent him, which was
crimson, with vellum button holes, bound
with Prussian binding: the captors then
conducted him to Lieutenant-Colonel Jamison, a continental officer, who had the
command of about nine hundred men, mostly
militia. When Major Andre was brought
before him, he passed under the name of
Anderson, choosing to hazard the greatest
danger rather than let any discovery be made
which could involve Arnold, before he had
time to provide for his safety. With this
view, to effect Arnold's escape, he requested that a line might be written to him,
to acquaint him with Anderson's detention,
which Jamison granted. The papers which

were found in the major's pocket-book, were
in Arnold's hand-writing, and contained exact returns of the state of the forces, ordnance, and defences, at West Point and
its dependencies, with the artillery orders,
critical remarks on the works, an estimate
of the number of men that were ordinarily
on duty to defend them, and a copy of a
state of affairs that had been laid before a
council of war, by the commander in chief,
on the 6th of the month. These papers
were enclosed in a packet to General Washington, accompanied with a letter from Ma·
jor Andre, avowing himself to be the adjutant-general of the British army, and was
forwarded by Jamison. Washington, at
that time, was upon his return from Hart-
ford, from his conference with Count Rochambeau, and the messenger missed him
by taking a different road from that on
which the general had gone. Through this
accident, and the man being obliged to make

a circuit, the letter to Arnold, informing
him of Anderson's capture, reached him a
short time before Washington's packet arrived at Robinson's house. Upon the re-
ceipt of it, Arnold seized the messenger's
horse, and instantly proceeded down a pre-
cipice, almost perpendicular, to the river,
where boats were always ready to pass to
and from West Point; he sprang into one,
and directed the hands to row him down the
river, and make for the Vulture; but he had
scarcely passed Stony and Verplank's Point,
when Colonel Hamilton arrived at the latter,
with orders to stop him; for by the time
Washington reached the house, the packet
from Jamison had arrived. Major Andre
had been three days in custody before Arnold's design was known in camp. Had it
succeeded, the consequence would have
been the termination of the war; for on the
loss of West Point, the troops under
Washington would have been exposed, with

the remainder of his army, to the united attack of the royal forces by land and water, and general ruin to the American cause must have been the result, as Washington would have been taken with the garrison, a circumstance which appears from his letter to a friend on that occasion, couched in the following terms :—" How far Arnold meant to involve me in the catastrophe of this place, does not appear by any indubitable evidence, and I am rather inclined to think he did not wish to hazard the more important object, by attempting to combine two events, the lesser of which might have marred the greater." He goes on to say, " a combination of extraordinary circumstances, an unaccountable depravation of mind in a man of the first abilities, and the virtue of three militia-men, threw the adjutant-general of the British forces (with full proof of Arnold's intention) into our hands; and but for the egregious folly, or the bewildered conception, of Lieutenant-Colonel Jamison, who seemed lost in astonishment, and not to have known what he was doing, I should have gotten Arnold."

But I must return to the situation of Major Andre. On the 25th of September General Washington appointed a board of fourteen general officers, (amongst whom was the Marquis de la Fayette and Baron De Stuben,) with the assistance of the judge-advocate, General John Lawrence, of whom I have before spoken, to examine into, and to report Major Andre's case, to form some judgment in what light he was to be considered, and to what punishment he was liable.

Major Andre, nobly disdaining to shield himself under any evasive subterfuge, and solely anxious to place his character in the fairest point of view, so as to prevent its

being discoloured by present or future circumstances, voluntarily declared more than
was required, and did not palliate any thing
relating to himself; while with the most
guarded caution, and the most scrupulous
nicety and circumspection, he concealed
whatever might criminate others. When
indirectly questioned respecting myself, he
generously answered, that he would fully
declare his sentiments, as they would have
more weight, from his own peculiar situation.
The candour and magnanimity of his conduct, united to the dignity of his deportment, while it struck his enemies with admiration, inspired an affecting tenderness
for his situation throughout the American
army.

On the 29th of September, the board of
general officers met, when a number of questions were proposed to him: the judge-advocate, who was by birth an Englishman,

and a gentleman of the greatest sensibility, was agitated with the tenderest emotion towards him, requested him not to hasten his replies to the interrogatories, nor to suffer his feelings to be embarrassed from the peculiarity of his situation ; and if the questions appeared to him to be worded with ambiguity, to demand a fair explanation of them, which should be granted. And here, before I proceed, I beg leave to mention, upon good authority, that it had been hinted to Major Andre by some of the officers who guarded him, or by some of General Washington's suite, that if he was demanded by Sir Henry Clinton in exchange, it was General Washington's determination to relinquish his prisoner. When Major Andre, on his capture, obtained leave to write to General Washington, he strongly urged that he could not by any means be considered as a spy ; these sentiments he maintained when brought to General Washington at Robertson's house. From the conversation which took place between Washington, the Marquis de la Fayette, and Major Andre, which I could plainly hear in the room wherein I was confined, Major Andre urged, that he came on shore under the sanction of a passport or flag of truce, transmitted to him by General Arnold, who was, at the time of granting it, a major-general in the American army, and, of course, had sufficient authority so to do, and " I clearly recollect the flag was sent to Colonel Beverly Robinson, Mr. John Anderson, or any other person they might authorize to return with me." As much dispute had arisen at the time in both the Royal and American armies, on the justice and propriety of executing a number of persons, whether they were as couriers, sanctioned by flags of truce, or came under the description of spies, it was generally conceived by the American army that the institution of this board of general

officers was for the purpose of fixing some
precise points to discriminate *these* characters, rather than seriously to try the major.
No precise charge was exhibited against
him ; the intention of the board, it was supposed, would be governed by the interrogatories before-mentioned and the answers to
them, in the decision of the major's case.
Baron De Stuben, who was one of the
board, opposed most of the general officers,
in their opinion that Major Andre ought to
be considered as a spy, upon the principle,
agreeably to the law of nations, as established by Grotius and Puffendorf, who,
as well as more modern authors on the subject, declare, that an enemy, having once
entered the lines of an enemy, or even the
fortress of an enemy, or his garrison, under
the sanction of a flag, the commanding officer of that garrison or fortress being at the
time authorized to grant such flag, his
personal safety becomes guaranteed from

violation, the moment a treaty is entered
into for the delivery of the garrison, whether the surrender of the garrison was to
be by treachery or otherwise.

From these premises the conclusion is
clear, that Major Andre came out under
every fair and justifiable sanction, and un-
questionably ought to have been returned
upon the demand of Sir Henry Clinton,
through the very humane interference of
Lieutenant-General James Robertson, pur-
posely appointed to solicit the release of the
adjutant-general, who was accompanied to
Dobbs' ferry by the governor of New York,
by Lieutenant-Governor Elliott, and Chief
Justice William Smith; that by their uniting
the military and civil powers, as both civil
and military characters were at that period
prisoners of war on both sides, any impediment to an exchange might be the more readily removed, and the horrors of war, as

much as possible, alleviated by a generous
system of reciprocation. Such a system
would have proved beneficial to the unhappy
prisoners on either side, who were at that
period deprived of those necessaries and consolations most dear to man. What I mention as the then sentiments of the amiable,
virtuous, and humane Baron De Stuben,
were certain declarations which he made in
company, when I was present, since the
war, and deplored his having been overruled by a majority of the board, so contrary
to his feelings of humanity, and sentiments
of justice.

Andre was fascinated by the alluring assurances which prefaced the judge-advocate's address to him, as well as by the
declarations given by the officers, servants,
and other attendants of General Washington;
but he was no less confident from the firm
ground on which he stood, he being invited on

shore by General Arnold, who had the same
power, in his own separate command, to give
him that invitation, agreeably to the resolve
of Congress, as General Washington himself; for surely no man had served his country, not even Washington, with more intrepidity, zeal, and fidelity; nor had he gained
more honourable applause, either in the army
of the United States, or among the citizens
at large.   It may be said, that the business
was of a traitorous nature, and of which
Major Andre was well informed : but if we
allow this to be the fact, it does not contra-
vene the general system, " that stratagems
are justifiable in war." If this were a crime,
the criminality rested on the officer who
made the defection, not on the gallant major who, in full uniform, in discharge of the
duty due to his king and country, boldly
went out to receive the terms and conditions
of a returning rebel to the allegiance of his
sovereign ; and in which return he was ac-

tuated by a sense of his former infamy, when injured by those who had refused justice to his claims, for faithful service, in *their* behalf, which had procured him nothing but broken limbs,and a debilitated constitution.

Here we see Major Andre, in the discharge of his duty, acting in obedience to his sovereign's proclamation, and the injunctions by his majesty's commissioners of 1778, engaged for pacification, namely, those amiable characters the Earl of Carlisle, Governor Johnston, and the benevolent and highly informed Lord Auckland, late president of the Board of Trade and Plantations. But the Marquis De Chastelleux, while he pays many compliments to the adjutant-general, in his Travels in 1780, 1781, 1782, and 1783, stiles him the *imprudent Andre :* on which I will only remark, that if the marquis was horror-stricken when passing over a small brook

H

near to, and after leaving my house in the
rear, plundered, forlorn, and destitute, by
that devastating spirit that has depopulated
half his own country, and decapitated the
sovereign he then served, it would be curi-
ous to know whether he thought *he* was *prudent*, to leave his own country, when in the
service of his king, and enrol himself in the
ranks of a faction, whose principles were
more demoniac than those of the murdering
Robespierre, or the insulting Corsican;
and more sanguinary than Cromwell's.
Major Andre, influenced by those sternly
noble principles, which animate the breast
of every virtuous freeman, thought no sacrifice dearly bought that could rescue two
countries, so blended by law, similarity of
manner, habit, consanguinity, and religion,
from the insidious rapacity of the Gallic
yoke.

The board of general officers having as-

sembled, in apparently solemn sanctity, by
reiteration of the same question in different
words and modifications of language, at
length extracted from the defenceless, friendless Andre something like a declaration that
he could not return on board the Vulture
under the sanction of the flag that had
brought him on shore, from whence they
inferred, he did not conceive himself under
the protection of that flag after he was once
landed within the American lines; nor indeed could he, from the reasons already
stated, namely, the change of dress, which
he declared, in his letter to Sir Henry Clinton, was imposed upon him, as well as
the mode of return. He generously for-
bore to assign to them the reasons which
had induced General Arnold, and which
Arnold had mentioned to him, to prefer
returning him by land to New York,
and also lest, by saying too much, he
might criminate others, for whose preser-

H 2

vation he appeared more solicitous than for
himself. No witnesses were adduced, nor
could any be brought who had the slightest
knowledge of the secret part of this transaction; of course, none were called; and the
board of general officers proceeded, after
making a statement of some facts, to wit,
that he had quitted his uniform which he had
worn under his surtout, for a coat given to
me in exchange for one of my own, a crimson broad cloth, vellum button holed, and
bound with Prussian binding; that he was
furnished with a horse, and, under the assumed name of John Anderson, with a passport from General Arnold, was proceeding
towards New York, when he was stopped
by John Paulding, David Williams, and
Isaac Van Vert, three of the New York
militia, who, with others, were scouting
between the out-posts of the two armies;
from which facts the board of general officers
proceeded to declare, " *That Major John*

Andre, adjutant-general of the British army, ought to be considered as a spy from the enemy, and that, agreeably to the law and usage of nations, it is their opinion he ought to suffer death.

This adjudication was passed on the 25th of September; Major Andre was captured on the 23d; General Arnold made his escape on the 25th; and on the 26th, Sir Henry Clinton wrote to General Washington to reclaim Major Andre. On the 30th, General Washington answered General Clinton; in his letter he says—" that though Major Andre was under such circumstances as would have justified the most summary proceeding against him, he had referred his case to the examination and decision of a board of general officers, whose report, founded on his free and voluntary confession of his letters, was inclosed."

Here I must remark, that the sentence of
the board of general officers was by no
means unanimous, and the letter *from Major Andre, assigning his reasons, why he
ought not to have been considered as a spy,
was not transmitted by General Washington.*
I refer to the letter that the major wrote
when under the custody of Colonel Jamison,
which placed Major Andre's character and
abilities in the most amiable point of view.

This letter from General Washington was
immediately answered by another from Sir
Henry Clinton, containing a proposition to
send General Robertson, with the gentlemen I mentioned, and requested Washington safely to conduct them to meet himself,
or whomsoever he should appoint, to give
him a statement of facts, and to explain Sir
Henry's sentiments on the subject. " He
urged it as a point of the highest concern to

humanity, that General Washington should
fully understand the whole state of the business, before he proceeded to carry the judgment of the board into execution."

General Greene, who had presided at this
board, was appointed to meet General Robertson. He had discovered the severest
malignity against Major Andre from the first
hour of his capture, and, in conjunction
with the Marquis de la Fayette, was determined to take his life; while La Fayette
publicly declared, that General Washington
himself deserved the halter, if he did not
apply it to the unfortunate Andre. Greene
met General Robertson at Dobbs's ferry;
the other two gentlemen before-mentioned
were not permitted to come on shore; for
the fact was, that their superior abilities,
virtue, and integrity of character, were well
known, and equally dreaded. It will not
be amiss here to take some notice of the

character, and the principles which assuredly influenced the conduct of General
Greene, though I am ready to give him all
the advantage of " *de mortuis nil nisi bonum*,"
which applies here as well to Major Andre
as himself, and also to many others in this
tragical drama, who now, in the energetic
language of Dr. Young, are " with the years
beyond the flood."

Yet this general rule of tenderness to the
frailties of human nature, adopted by philan-
thropists, if attended to, respects the dead,
while it injures the living, by preventing
posterity from having the light of biogra-
phical experience; for surely it is wisdom to
regulate life by the sage conduct of those
whose career in the' various parts of it has
been stamped with honourable applause, or
has been degraded by merited infamy. It
was a fixed system with General Washington " to take the passions of men as nature

had given them, and those principles as a
guide, which are generally the rule of action." General Greene was of the quaker
persuasion, although a military man; a lu-
dicrous contradiction; for that sect are well
known to possess an aversion to arms; yet
General Greene took to the field, and
none of the American officers displayed a
more martial spirit than himself, except General Arnold. General Greene, from the
first, viewed Arnold's rapid advancement
and military achievements with envy, and I
have witnessed with no small concern, when
in company with them both, that " *splene-
tic cordiality*," as Sterne expresses the idea,
which is the eternal companion of compe-
titors, ambitious for renown.

It was well known that General Greene's
mind, previous to engaging in the service of
his country, was distempered by one of the
most painful domestic calamities, that could

agonise the soul of a man of spirit. This ostensible misery had followed him to the camp at Orange Town; too many flagrant proofs had blunted the edge of those fine feelings known only to sympathetic spirits, drawn irresistibly by the silken ties of disinterested affection; approved by reason, cemented by love; sanctioned by virtue, and applauded by angels: General Greene, in short, was chagrined by the comparative happiness which his competitor for fame enjoyed, in obtaining the amiable Miss Shippen, of Philadelphia, of which city she was the ornament and pride.

By every insinuating address he courted the favour of General Washington, who appointed him to the presidency of this board of general officers, in preference to General Robert Howe, a gentleman and a philanthropist, who was not calculated for conniving at the murdering *decree*. Indeed,

the defection of General Arnold was so
great a surprise, that General Washington
knew not in whom to confide, each of his
officers being envious of the other, and suspicions engendered by former jealousies
spread abroad, while Pandora's poisonous
box was opened for their reception: General
Greene availed himself of every malignant,
deadly mischief flowing from it, and im•
proved the occasion to manifest his fatal de-
terminations. This general was therefore
selected and appointed for the interview with
General Robertson; who, by the clearest
reasoning, demonstrated that Major Andre
did not come under the character or description of a spy, and proposed that General
Knyphausen, of the auxiliary troops, in the
service of his Britannic Majesty, on the one
part, and General Count Rochambeau, as
not so immediately interested, should be
consulted, and their opinions taken on a
subject so interesting to the cause of huma-

nity. General Robertson, indeed, made
use of every argument to induce a re-consideration of Major Andre's case; but the
proposed reference was not acceded to by
General Washington. He quoted and proved
many instances of Sir Henry Clinton's mer-
ciful inclination of mind, in cases where,
upon similar applications, Sir Henry had
softened the rigorous severities of war; and,
in the most impressive language, urged the
necessity of adopting a reciprocal disposition
of amity, as most compatible with the genuine spirit of real bravery; offering, on
the discharge of Major Andre, to engage
that any person whatever, in the custody of
the opposite party, should be immediately
restored to his liberty; adding, that Sir
Henry Clinton entertained a high esteem
for Major Andre, and wished an interchange
of such civilities, as would lay himself under the most permanent obligations; in short,
every persuasion that could be urged, was

resorted to by General Robertson, that could
excite the commiseration of any other man
but General Greene, who even refused to
deliver the purport of General Robertson's
proposal of vesting the decision as recited,
or of mentioning any of the arguments adduced by Robertson to General Washington.
Such unfeeling apathy might, however, have
been anticipated by those who knew the
unfeeling principles by which that general
was influenced.

No gentleman, perhaps, possessed the
powers of persuasion in a more eminent degree than Lieutenant-General Robertson.
He was a Scotchman, a native of Fifeshire;
and with the firm integrity of his countrymen, he united the experience of a veteran,
in policy and military knowledge.   His
adroit and perspicuous answers, when examined before the House of Commons,
were at once a display of his abilities as a

soldier, and of his inflexible loyalty as a
Briton. The wisdom of government was
never more demonstrated than in his appointment to the chief civil authority as governor of New York, that city having been
Lieutenant-General Robertson's residence
since the pacification of 1760. He was
well known and equally beloved by the inhabitants of the province; and when colonel
of his majesty's 16th regiment of foot, during the troubles that agitated the minds of
the inhabitants, in consequence of their dis-
contents, arising from the stamp and other
acts of parliament, which were deemed obnoxious, he invariably was the mediator
between the civil and military powers.
Hence, by his wisdom and discreet deportment, a spirit of harmony was cultivated
and maintained; and there never was a governor appointed by the crown, who more
fully possessed the hearts of the people, except Governor Clinton, the father of Sir

Henry Clinton, the commander in chief, who was the idol of the province. This fact is mentioned in Chief Justice Smith's History of New York. Lieutenant-General Robertson, with such abilities, of course, became the most eligible person for a mission of so humane and political a nature, uniting in his person the civil and military characters, which well qualified him to effect the exchange in the proposal solicited by Sir Henry Clinton.

By the long residence of General Robertson in New York, he was well acquainted with the canting disposition and character of his Eastern neighbours, who, having incessantly the sound of religion on the tongue, as a mask more effectually to deceive and surprise the unwary, are never really known until deception discovers their hypocrisy.

Upon General Robertson's departure from General Greene, he pathetically urged the re-consideration of the subject of their interview. But Greene being determined not to alter the decision of the board of general officers, of which he was president, did not relate to Washington the particulars of the interview, which, in the then state of General Washington's mind, would have saved the life of Major Andre, or, at least, would have mitigated the punishment. For this apathetic and inhuman silence, Congress effectually remunerated Greene, by giving him a valuable plantation, in the state of Georgia, the meed of his indefatigable services, but which was, ultimately, his bane, and the cause of his premature death; for depending too much upon his hardy constitution, contrary to the advice of his friends, he would, to accomplish the duties, and acquire the simple character of a planter, venture out, and subject himself to the meridian blaze of the sun, in order to super-intend his negro labourers: in one of these perambulations he received the " *coup de so-liel,*" or, stroke of the sun, as the French West Indians term the effects which Euro-peans feel from too great an exertion, while subjected to the solar heat; and fell a victim to his own obstinacy, unrelented by some, and deplored by others; for political attach-ments bore their preponderance in that un-happy, divided, and distracted country, till the last hour of the unfortunate war; and even now they are far, very far, from ex-tinction. In the minds of some this general still lives, and is considered as the *deputy-saviour* of his country. Hosanna one hour, and crucify the next, was the prevailing prin-ciple among the Americans! " *Sic transit gloria mundi!* "

The malignity, virulence, and savage bar-

I

barity that, at the above-mentioned time, pervaded all ranks, classes, and denominations, whether in the civil or military line, cannot be delineated in any terms but such as must agonise the heart of sensibility, and cause a blush on the cheek of civilised humanity.; and the baneful effects of which were not eradicated so late as the year 1801. When, at a place called Ninety Six, and at Augusta, in Georgia, in a large company, among the gentry of the country, where, it would be supposed, humanity would prevail, were it only through decency, and with a view to example, I heard them boast of having committed barbarities shocking to human nature. One instance was that of an old, grey-headed justice of the peace, who solemnly declared he had, during the war, shot, at different actions, and in cold blood, ninety-nine Tories, and felt unhappy he had not accomplished the complete hundred! Shocked at the ferocity of this sanguinary

monster, I pressed my friend and fellow-traveller to make a precipitate departure, although we had rode a great distance that
day, and were both fatigued and hungry;
he was of my opinion, and we therefore left
the cannibal-justice to try some causes
which, he said, would afford some sport,
being only a few bastardies, rapes, and similar trifles, as he termed them; indeed, before we got off, he went to the full fruition
of his mirth, the bottle and the bible, inse-
parable companions in that country, during
their summary modes of adjudication! We
were, in fact, happy in escaping from the
sight and association of beings abhorrent
to human nature; and hastened towards
Augusta, in Georgia. I cannot pass over a
circumstance that happened at this latter
place, which excited some merriment, as a
contrast to the anecdote I have just related.

A Connecticut merchant is the denomination applied individually to a set of people who, in the autumnal months, leave Connecticut river, and, in small sloops, schooners, or shallops, run down the continent, laden with onions, apples, cyder, potatoes, and sometimes New England rum and pork, having little more nautical skill than that of ascertaining the direction of the coast, keeping within soundings, and carefully avoiding the stream, which constantly runs from the Gulph of Mexico to the Banks of Newfoundland.   One of these merchants had reached Savannah, the capital of Georgia, and finding the market glutted with what he called his *corn* customers, honest Nathan * was advised to try his market at Au-

* I hope the reader will not suspect that I mean by this anecdote any reflections on the character of the quakers—far from it.   In this country, in particular, they are an ornament to their profession ; and, perhaps, the most consistent people, as a body, that America can boast of.

gusta, in Georgia, then the seat of government, under the administration of Governor
Tellfair. The merchant's name was Nathan
Putnam, a near relation of the celebrated
General Putnam, who, with Doctor War-
ren, of Boston, so vigorously defended Bun-
ker's Hill, in 1775, against the British troops,
in the Massachuset government. Merchant
Putnam had applied to a Mr. Longstreet, a
native of Prince Town, New Jersey, to pur-
chase his cargo of combustibles,—a bargain
was struck; but the merchant not having
delivered the combustibles within the time
limited by the contract, a dispute arose;
when Longstreet, who hated the New England people, whom he termed Yankies, was
determined to seize the goods, as forfeited by
the contract, and apply them to his own
use; he therefore armed a party to effect his
purpose, who, having drunk very freely of
the hard, strong cider, which is called
wring-jaw-cider, from its being boiled down

and distilled, they proceeded to seize merchant Putnam; and the more effectually to
gain their point, some of them declared he
was the identical Benedict Arnold, who had
confederated to give up West Point to the
British, and had come there in disguise. It
being in the twilight, and the merchant re-
sembling in size and appearance the general
alluded to, the report was instantly believed,
and the poor merchant being seized, in vain
denied the charge, and appealed to many
persons as to the identity of his person.
They were actually proceeding to tar and
roll him in a bed of feathers, and from
thence to throw him into the Savannah
river, when he was fortunately known by his
voice to a Colonel Dorsey, and with much
difficulty recovered by the colonel, who had
been at his father's house during the war,
when in the continental service; while,
being a quaker, he merely affirmed he was
not the real Benedict Arnold, having served

under that general in his march from the
camp at Cambridge to the walls of Quebec.
The interference of Colonel Dorsey, however, would have been of no avail, had he
not been highly and deservedly respected,
as a gentleman of liberality, courage, and
influence.   Hearing the tumultuous uproar,
I was proceeding to enquire into the cause,
when I was met by Colonel Dorsey, with
whom I became acquainted in England soon
after the American war, and who, knowing
my precarious situation, was coming forward, from political reasons, to warn me of
my danger; on our meeting, he strongly
urged my departure, lest any suspicion
should arise, which might prove injurious
to my personal safety.

Being acquainted with the governor's lady,
whom I knew in 1774, and having brought
letters of recommendation to the governor,
from his friends in Charleston, with whom

I had frequently dined in company with the people of the first distinction in the country; the legislature then sitting, and it being also the sitting of the supreme court of judicature for the state, accompanied with the usual commission of oyer and terminer, I was not intimidated by the gentlemen of the mobility ; in fact, I wished to hear the debates, and the new mode of administering justice. It was, however, a friendly caution on the part of Colonel Dorsey, and which I found, on adherence to it, of great utility to me, in travelling through the continent in general; and in this instance particularly, for the fracas just mentioned had revived the malevolence of party; and the whole history of General Arnold's defection from the American cause became again the subject of detail. I have sat in public companies, have been on the road travelling, *incognito*, and heard myself almost as severely execrated as an accomplice with General Arnold, and as much threatened, as he himself could possibly be, if he were to fall into their hands. Such incidents forcibly brought to my remembrance an expression of General Washington to my friend Colonel Hay, when I was under my trial for life, viz. " that we may as well hang him as not, for he can never be happy if acquitted." It is somewhat remarkable, that he never published the sentence of the court-martial which, for six weeks, was employed in my trial, thereby intending to fix a stigma that, he conceived, would embitter my future life. I am confident that he anxiously meditated my destruction ; but, being favoured by the law, and the hand of Divine Providence, which sustained me under my severe afflictions, I was enabled to offer a defence, that baffled every attempt to cause me to suffer the tragical fate of the lamented Andre:—Yet Washington would have attempted my de-

struction, had he not been dissuaded by
General Greene, on account of the insuffici-
ency of the evidence, and the influence of
his lady, (of whom I shall have occasion
to speak hereafter,) as well as from a special
regard which General Greene bore towards
a favourite nephew, Lieutenant-Colonel
William Livingston, of Colonel Webb's
regiment of Continentals, who fought under
his command at Rhode Island, in the year
1779; he therefore affectionately interested
himself in my behalf. The very handsome
manner in which General Greene spoke of
this young and gallant officer, as well as of
Colonel Henry B. Livingston, who were
both in this action, did him great honour;
his eulogium being strictly true, and much
less than the objects of it, from all circumstances, deserved.

From the cool and intrepid conduct of
General Greene at Rhode Island, at the pe-

riod above-mentioned, and the combinations and intrigues of Generals Gates, Miflin, and others, against General Washington, he became more closely attached to General Greene than any officer under his command, and was supposed instrumental in the disgraceful act of superseding General Gates, by the appointment of General Greene to the command of the American southern army ; and from that period they seemed to be actuated by one common interest, which clearly accounts for that unison of design, which was evident in the conduct of the commander in chief and the president of the board instituted by the former, for the fate of the unfortunate adjutant-general.

When General Robertson left General Greene at Dobbs's ferry, and returned to the gentlemen who accompanied him in the flag of truce, he was not without hopes that some remaining principle of humanity, or

spark of tenderness, which General Greene
had discovered, when the purport of the interview was related to the chieftain, might
excite a spirit of clemency towards many
that might otherwise fall victims to rigorous
severity,* in the further prosecution of the
war.   But he was mistaken ; for as he came
resolved to withstand all entreaties of humanity, so he was determined not to suggest to
his principal any matter that might excite
remorse in his mind, but, on the contrary,
like another Iago, festered the wound that
he had opened.   A furious letter from General Arnold, replete with threats in case
Major Andre should suffer under the sentence of the board of general officers,
charging General Washington with being
answerable for all the bloodshed consequent
on that event, increased the flame.   This

* A large number of the citizens of South Carolina
had virtually forfeited their lives at this time, and yet
were spared by Sir Henry Clinton.

letter added fuel to the rancourous enmity
he entertained against his ancient rival, and
tended rather to precipitate the deplored
event, or, at least, to make it the more in-
evitable; while General Robertson was cen-
sured for, what was termed, the absurdity
of presenting it.

From the 25th of September, the day of
the appointment of the board of officers by
General Washington, to the 5th of October,
was passed in the transmission of flags on
this unhappy subject, during which time
Major Andre calmly composed his mind
with philosophic, but rather with Christian
fortitude, preparing for whatever might be
the event of the negociation, which he understood was making in his behalf: but he
was at length informed that the die was cast,
and his destiny irretrievable, conformably to
the usage of war annexed to his sentence.
He then wrote to his most worthy friend

and patron, Sir Henry Clinton, in language which no pen could surpass; and also a letter to General Washington, replete with all the dignified sentiment of a man of honour, and with all the pathos of a man of the finest feelings, earnestly requesting that he might die as a soldier, and not as a malefactor; to which, however, no reply was made. The following is the letter last alluded to :

" *Tappan, Oct.* 1, 1780.

" Sir,

" Buoyed above the terror of death, by the consciousness of a life devoted to honourable pursuits, and stained with no action that can give me remorse, I trust that the request I make to your excellency at this serious period, and which is to soften my last moments, will not be rejected.

" Sympathy towards a soldier will surely

induce your excellency, and a military tribunal, to adapt the mode of my death to the feelings of a man of honour.

" Let me hope, Sir, that if aught in my character impresses you with esteem towards me, if aught in my misfortunes marks me as the victim of policy, and not of resentment, I shall experience the operation of these feelings in your breast, by being informed that I am not to die on a gibbet.

" I have the honour to be,

your excellency's most obedient,

and most humble servant,

JOHN ANDRE,

Adjutant-General to the

British Army."

During all this period, from the time of our being conducted from West Point, the 26th of September, to the 30th, I was closely guarded in the church of Tappan, or

Orange Town, and there were not wanting
those who gave me intimations of the plans
that were formed against the life of Major
Andre, as well as the engines that were at
work against myself; and I shall ever retain,
in grateful remembrance, the tender and
sympathising consolations, which I received
from a very young gentleman of the name of
Edwards, from Massachuset's-Bay government, who often commanded the guard,
under whose care I was confined. The most
virtuous and worthy of the aged inhabitants
of the county of Orange did not fail to visit
me on this occasion; and particularly the
good Judge Cove, of Kakiat, Judge Heron,
and Abraham Thew, Esq. a man who had
served his country with the most unexam-
pled zeal and fidelity, during the Canadian
war, which terminated in the peace of
1763, and who, as a reward for his prowess
and gallantry, was so highly complimented
by the friend of my family, the late Lord

Jeffery Amherst, whose memory will live
in the annals of military virtue and honour.

My turn was now to commence, and, on
the day appointed for my trial, the judge-
advocate, by order of General Washington,
who was prosecutor, exhibited ten separate
charges against me, so artfully drawn up, that
the proof of one would necessarily involve,
as by inference, some testimony to support
the other. Aware of the snare which was
laid for me, I requested that the charges
might be consolidated into one general ac-
cusation. Accordingly, on the ensuing
day, when the court was convened, this
request was granted; and I was ordered to
answer to the following charge, with the
usual ceremonial :—

" You stand charged with aiding and assisting Benedict Arnold, late a major-general
in our service, in a combination with the

K

enemy, for the purpose of taking, seizing, and killing such of the loyal citizens and soldiers of these United States, as were in garrison at West Point, and its dependencies."

In answer to this charge, I objected to the legality, or propriety, of being tried by a military tribunal; for, as a citizen, I conceived myself only amenable to the civil authority of the state, to which I belonged, which had established the right of trial by jury in the constitution recently adopted, determining the liberties of the subjects within the state, and had ordained " That the right of trial by jury, in all cases wherein it had been formerly used in the colony of New York, should be, and remain, inviolate for ever." I was answered by the court, that I was tried by a resolve of congress, passed in the year 1777, authorizing the commander in chief of the army, to hear and

try by court-martial, any of the citizens of
the United States, who should harbour or
secret any of the subjects or soldiers of the
King of Great Britain, knowing them to be
such, or should be instrumental in conveying intelligence to the enemy, and, if found
guilty, should be condemned and executed
as a traitor, assassin, and spy. To this I
objected, that the resolve of Congress just
alluded to, was possibly passed anterior to
the adoption of the several constitutions of
the United States, when there were no legal
establishments, and was introduced to supply the want of civil jurisdictions in that
early stage of the war; and that I could
not conceive how a mere resolve of congress could abrogate a fundamental article
in any of the civil constitutions of the
United States; for, if so, it made the military paramount to the civil authority, and
would establish, if the court were to proceed
on my trial, a precedent dangerous to the

liberties of the subject; that it would excite
eventually the indignation of my fellow-
citizens, in destroying one of the established
principles of liberty belonging to the subject,
and the violation of the right of trial by
jury, one of the principal reasons assigned
by congress for their separation from Great
Britain, in the declaration of independence,
as well as allowing the military an extent
of power incompatible with a free government.

The court, however, after having with-
drawn some time for consultation, overruled my objections, and proceeded to examine the evidence in support of the prosecutor's charge.

The first that were produced, were the
Marquis de la Fayette, General Knox, and
Colonels Harrison and Hamilton; the pur-
port of whose testimony was, my declara-

tion to General Hamilton, when brought
before him at Robinson's house from Fish
Kill.   In giving their evidence separately,
they each deviated from the other, although
they were all present at the time of examination before the court-martial.

General Knox and Colonel Hamilton came,
in testimony, more pointed to the exact truth
of what I had declared, especially the latter,
whose evidence was perfectly correct, by
which was anticipated what must have been
otherwise extracted in cross-examination ;
yet Hamilton artfully threw in a chain of
reasoning, tending to prove my being in full
knowledge of General Arnold's intentions.
Harrison's testimony was imperfect on the
most material points, as he detailed those
parts that militated against me in support of
the charge, and excluded those that favoured my life ; for, in all these cases, a
man's declaration should be taken connec-

tively, and not be detached; otherwise, by
selecting some parts, and rejecting others,
in support of a charge, it must be evident
that the most innocent man may be made to
contradict, and even to condemn himself.

The Marquis de la Fayette was most
widely different in his testimony from the
rest of these gentlemen; he delivered his
evidence with acrimonious severity, and
malignant bitterness: he asserted as part of
my declaration to General Washington matters that I could not have mentioned; and
had my life, or that of a hundred others,
depended on his credibility before an ignorant court-martial, all would have been forfeited.

I had paid particular attention to the testimony of General Knox and Colonel Hamilton, in my notes taken on their evidence;
and in my cross-examination of the marquis,

I applied their answers and remarks to his recollection, which did not a little embarrass him. I could plainly perceive the court-martial were sensible that he was mistaken; and I most sincerely hope he erred from ignorance of the true import of the English language.

The avowed enmity which the marquis entertained against General Arnold, induced him to take vengeance on all who were supposed to be in the least degree connected with him, and there were so many presumptive circumstances which favoured my being of that complexion, that they in some measure account for his vindictiveness. Previous to this event, we had been on good terms; but he left the court-martial much chagrined, and I understood from one of General Washington's domestics, who daily brought me provisions, and who was a confidential servant of the general's, that the marquis, on all occasions, when my name was mentioned, expressed himself with great asperity.

The next evidences that were produced, were Samuel and Joseph Colquhoun, the boatmen, who rowed me on board the Vulture; the three militia-men, who captured Major Andre; and the ferry-men, who conveyed us from Stony to Verplank's Point.

The two boatmen corroborated the substance of what I had declared to General Washington, on my first arrest, with a number of other circumstances, which were of little or no consequence, excepting their acknowledging their total inability of returning Major Andre to the Vulture, after landing him at the Long Clove, for his conference with General Arnold, through the excessive fatigue they had undergone already, and from the change of the tide. I will only

here remark, that I was aware of this impracticability, when I left the Vulture, and
had solicited the addition of two hands from
the captain, which were refused, but from
what motives I cannot determine, unless for
the reasons I have already suggested, that
there appeared no concert of design between
the military and naval departments; and
yet it has since appeared that the Vulture
was stationed in the bay of Haverstraw pur-
posely to promote the measures that were in
agitation.

These two men delivered their evidence
with a plainness, perspicuity, and firmness,
that seemed to have much weight with the
court-martial, who examined them with
critical scrutiny.   After the judge-advocate
had finished the examination, they were the
most material evidences that could be adduced.   I will just mention the disgraceful
means that were used to impeach the inte-

grity of the eldest Samuel Colquhoun, from
which circumstance it will appear in what a
precarious situation my life was placed.

There is now a person in this kingdom,
who was informed by Samuel Colquhoun,
that while I was on my trial, he was taken
into a field by some of General Washington's
officers, who read to him a paper purporting
to be a declaration of the means which I
had adopted, and which if he would attest
against me on the trial, he should have a
purse of gold, which was then offered to him,
and a promise of support for life;—Colquhoun answered, that although he was a poor
man, he could not swear falsely for money,
which he should do if he attested the paper;
and, if made rich by such means, he added,
that he should be miserable for life.

The next evidence adduced was Colonel
Hay, who accompanied me from his house

at Fish Kill to Robinson's house, when
under the guard of ·Colonel Govion, the
amount of which was, my declaration to
him of the nature of my agency with General Arnold.   His testimony differed very
little in substance from the declaration made
to General Washington, as related by the
four first witnesses, General Knox, &c.

The next evidences were the ferrymen,
who proved that I had conducted Major
Andre across the posts of Stony and Verplank's Point, and mentioned some desultory conversation that had passed, but
which, at this period, can be of no consequence; they, however, deposed, that there
appeared to them an intimacy between Major Andre and myself, that was of a very
long standing.

These evidences were followed by the
three militia-men, who had stopped and

captured Major Andre, and with them were produced the papers which, they said, were found in Major Andre's boot: the names of these men were Paulding, Van Vert, and Williams.

Upon their being individually desired to depose what they knew, or could declare concerning me, they each said they had never seen me before; but upon its being suggested that my name was mentioned in some of the papers found upon Major Andre, the papers were read, and were to the following purpose :—

Artillery Orders, Sept. 5, 1780.

Estimate of the Force at West Point, and its Dependencies, Sept. 1780.

Estimate of Men to defend the Works at West Point, &c.

Return of Ordnance at West Point, Sept. 1780.

Remarks on the Works at West Point.

Copy of a State of Matters, laid before a Council of War, by his Excellency General Washington, held the 6th of Sept. 1780.

A letter, signed John Anderson, dated the 7th of September, 1780, to Colonel Sheldon, was also laid before the court-martial, which, the judge-advocate said, had been shewn to Major Andre, who acknowledged to have written it, and which was as follows:—

"*New York, Sept.* 1, 1780.

" SIR,

" I am told my name is made known to you, and that I may hope your indulgence in permitting me to meet a friend near our posts. I will endeavour to obtain permission to go out with a flag, which is to be sent to Dobbs's Ferry, on Monday next, the 11th, when I shall be happy to meet Mr. G——. Should I not be allowed to

go, the officer, who is to command the
escort, between whom and myself no distinction need be made, can speak on the
affair; let me intreat you, Sir, to favour a
matter so interesting to the parties concerned, and which is of so private a nature,
that the public on neither side can be injured by it.

" I shall be happy, on my part, in doing
any act of kindness to you in a family or
property concern of a similar nature.

" I trust I shall not be detained; but
should any old grudge be a cause for it, I
should rather risk that, than neglect the
business in question, or assume a myste-
rious character to carry on an innocent affair; and, as friends have advised, get your
lines by stealth.

" I am, Sir, with all regard,

your most humble servant,

Col. Sheldon.   JOHN ANDERSON."

In addition to the papers found on Major Andre, there was produced the pass, given to him by General Arnold, to go to the White Plains, (which was a distance about half way between Pine's Bridge and New York, and to proceed, if he thought fit, as far as New York.

There was also another paper, containing a list of a number of persons living in the vicinity of the posts of Stony and Verplank's Points; in this list my name was inserted, which was read to me, and I was called upon to declare for what purpose it was placed among the preceding inclosures? As I knew many of the persons mentioned, and that they were of very opposite political principles, I could give no decisive answer, and as it did not apply to me, I said I conceived none was necessary on my part, for no man was bound to say that legally which might condemn himself. I therefore left the court-martial to place what construction they pleased on that paper, and, indeed, upon the whole of them, asserting at the time, that not being a military man, I knew nothing about their nature.

When Major Andre was under his trial before the board of general officers, these papers were produced against him, as appears from an extract of their proceedings, in a letter transmitted by General Washington to Congress, and afterwards published by them under the signature of Charles Thompson, their secretary, agreeably to their order.

It appears from these extracts, that when the above letter was read to Major Andre, he nobly avowed his being the author, as all stratagems in war are justifiable; but he delivered to the board these impressive sentiments,—"That this letter could be of no force in the case in question, as it was written in New York, when he was under the orders of General Clinton, but that it tended to prove, that it was not his intention to come within our lines."

It may not be amiss here to exhibit the letter which Major Andre addressed to General Washington, from Salem, dated the 24th of September, 1780, after he was sent across the country in West Chester, and placed in Colonel Sheldon's care, from the custody of Colonel Jamison. This letter communicates his sentiments in a clear point of view, and is too interesting to be passed over in silence, it being totally repugnant to what the board of general officers mention as Major Andre's confession to them, on which they justify their sentence:

" SIR,

" What I have as yet said concerning

L

myself, was in the justifiable attempt to be extricated; I am too little accustomed to duplicity to have succeeded.

" I beg your excellency to be persuaded, that no alteration in the temper of my mind, or apprehension for my safety, induces me to the step of addressing you; but that it is to secure myself from an imputation of having assumed a mean character for treacherous purposes or self-interest; a conduct incompatible with the principles that actuated me, as well as with my condition in life.

" It is to vindicate my fame I speak, and not to solicit security.

" The person in your possession is Major Andre, Adjutant-general of the British army.

" The influence of one commander, in

the army of his adversary, is an advantage taken in war. A correspondence for this purpose I held as confidential (in the present instance,) with his excellency Sir Henry Clinton.

" To favour it, I agreed to meet, upon ground not within the posts of either army, a person who was to give me intelligence; I came up in the Vulture sloop of war for this effect, and was fetched by the boat from the ship to the beach; being there I was told the approach of day would prevent my return, and that I must be concealed until the next night. I was in my regimentals, and had fairly risked my person.

" Against my stipulation, my intention, and without my knowledge before-hand, I was conducted within one of your posts. Your excellency may conceive my sentiments on this occasion, and will imagine

how much more I must have been affected
by a refusal to re-conduct me back the next
night as I had been brought; thus become a
prisoner, I had to concert my escape; I
quitted my uniform, and was passed another
way in the night, without the American
posts, to neutral ground; and being informed
I was out of the reach of all armed parties,
and left to proceed for New York, I was
taken at Tarry Town by some volunteers.

" Thus, as I have had to relate, I was
betrayed (being adjutant-general of the British army) into the vile condition of an enemy
within your posts.

" Having avowed myself a British officer,
I know nothing to reveal but what relates to
myself, which is true on the honour of an
officer and a gentleman.

·' The request I have to make to your ex-

cellency, and I am conscious I address myself well, is, that in any rigour policy may
dictate, a decency of conduct towards me
may mark that, though unfortunate, I am
branded with nothing dishonourable, as no
motive could be mine, but the service of
my king, and as I was involuntarily an im-
postor.

" Another request is, that I may be permitted to write an open letter to Sir Henry
Clinton, and another to a friend for clothes
and linen.

" I take the liberty to mention the condition of some gentlemen at Charleston, who,
being either on parole, or under protection,
were engaged in a conspiracy against us;
though their situation is not similar, they are
objects who may be sent in exchange for
me, or are persons, whom the treatment I
receive, may in some degree affect.

" It is no less, Sir, a confidence in the generosity of your mind, than on account of
your superior station, that I have chosen to
importune you with this letter.—I have the
honour to be, with the greatest respect, Sir,

   " Your excellency's most obedient,

         and most humble servant,

 " *His Excellency*   JOHN ANDRE,

Geo. Washington, &c."   *Adjt. Gen.*"

I must here request the candid reader's
peculiar attention to the manly, generous,
and undisguised sentiments of this unfortunate British officer.

Here is an explicit avowal of his object,
and the truly justifiable means which he
pursued to obtain it,—justifiable in every
sense, provided stratagems in war, by the
law of belligerent nations, be admissible,
and daily public accounts of military exploits
prove the position.

I carried the flag from General Arnold to
the Vulture, for any person to venture himself on shore.   It was addressed " To Colonel Beverly Robinson, John Anderson, or
whomsoever they might depute." This
fact was attested by the two boatmen who
rowed me on board the Vulture, and was
the purport of the paper which I shewed to
the court martial on my trial, in my own
vindication, as being under the direction of
General Arnold.   On this point, when produced, they seemed to relax in their virulence against me; for, by the powers vested
in general officers, commanding separate dis-
tricts of sixty miles around their distinct
commands, the citizen, as well as the soldier,
was, as I mentioned before, amenable to all
the penalties of martial law, by the order of
Congress, who, in the exigency of affairs,
even dispensed with defined constitutional
principles, in the unalienable rights of citizenship.   And yet this board of general of-

ficers, because there was at that time no aid
to assist Major Andre, availing themselves
of trespass on this common benefit, destroyed his life with impunity.

It is requisite to observe, that General
Washington, speaking of the letter which I
have just recited, in one that he wrote to
Congress, dated September 25, 1780, upon
the first discovery of Arnold's defection,
expresses himself to this effect: after mentioning that he had returned from Hertford,
to join his command at Robinson's house,
he savs,—" I arrived here yesterday, about
twelve o'clock. Some hours previous to my
arrival, Major-General Arnold went from
his quarters, which were at this place, and,
as it was supposed, over the river, to the
garrison at West Point, whither I proceeded
myself, in order to visit the posts. I found
General Arnold had not been there during
the day ; and, on my return to his quarters,

he was still absent. In the mean time, a
packet had arrived from Lieutenant-Colonel Jamison, announcing the capture of
John Anderson, who was endeavouring to
go to New York, with several interesting
and important papers, all in the hand-
writing of General Arnold. This was accompanied by a letter from the prisoner,
avowing himself to be Major John Andre,
adjutant-general of the British army, *relating the manner of his capture, and endeavouring to shew he did not come under
the description of a spy*. From these several
circumstances, and information that the
general seemed to be thrown into some degree of agitation, on receiving a letter a
little before he went from his quarters, I
was led to conclude immediately that he
had heard of Major Andre's captivity, and
that he would, if possible, escape to the
enemy, and accordingly took such measures as appeared most probable to appre-

hend him, but he had embarked in a barge, and proceeded down the river under a flag, to the Vulture sloop of war, which lay some miles distant below Stony and Verplank's Point. He wrote me a letter after he got on board. Major Andre has not arrived yet, but I hope he is secure, and that he will be here to-morrow. I have been, and am taking precautions, which I hope will prove effectual, to prevent the important consequences, which this conduct on the part of General Arnold was intended to produce," &c.

It is apparent, by his letter to General Washington, that Major Andre did not consider himself in the character of a spy, for so General Washington understood the import of his sentiments; and when the hands that rowed me to the Vulture were pressed to return him, Major Andre himself, upon their mentioning that the ship would be fired upon at day-break, said in reply, "*you can reach the ship, and be far enough, before that can happen, and the same flag that carried you to the ship, will make you safe on your return to General Arnold's command.*"

That Major Andre was under the protection of a flag, appears from General Arnold's letter to Sir Henry Clinton, dated New York, Sept. 26, 1780, of which the following is a copy :—

" SIR,

" IN answer to your excellency's message, respecting your adjutant-general Major Andre, and delivering my ideas of the reason why he is detained, being under my passports, I have the honour to inform you I apprehend a few hours must return Major Andre to your excellency's orders, as that officer is assuredly under the protection of a flag of truce, sent by me to him, for the purpose of a conversation I requested to hold with him relating to myself, and which I wished to communicate to that officer or to your excellency.

" I commanded at the time at West Point, and had an undoubted right to send my flag of truce for Major Andre, who came to me under that protection; and having held my conversation with him, I delivered to him confidential papers in my own hand-writing, to deliver to your excellency. Thinking it much properer he should return by land, I directed him to make use of the feigned name of John Anderson, under which he had, by my direction, come on shore, and gave him my passports for his safe return to your excellency; all which I had a right then to do, being in the actual service of America, under the orders of Ge-

neral Washington, and commanding general
at West Point, and its dependencies.

" I have the honour to be,
        your excellency's most obedient
            and very humble servant,
" *His Excellency*   B. ARNOLD."
Sir Henry Clinton."

In unison with the same sentiment, Colonel Beverly Robinson thus expressed himself in his letter to General Washington, dated
" Vulture, off Sinsink, Sept, 25, 1780,"
and he saw the flag I brought on board :—

" SIR,

" I am this moment informed, that Major Andre, adjutant-general of the British
army in America, is detained as a prisoner
by the army under your command.

" It is therefore incumbent on me to inform you of the manner of his falling into

your hands:—He went up with a flag at the request of General Arnold, on public business with him, and had his permit to return by land to New York. Upon these circumstances, Major Andre cannot be detained by you, without the greatest violation of flags, and contrary to the customs and usage of all nations; and as I imagine you will see this in the same manner as I do, I must desire you will order him to be set at liberty. Every step Major Andre took, was by the advice and direction of General Arnold, even that of taking a feigned name, and, of course, not liable to answer for it.

"I am, Sir,

not forgetting our former acquaintance,

your very humble servant,

BEVERLEY ROBINSON,

Col. Roy. Americans."

" *His Excellency*

General Washington."

In consequence of these facts, and agreeably to the opinion of the most experienced
officers in the garrison of New York, who
deemed it consistent with the laws of nations, as established by the most eminent
writers on the subject, Sir Henry Clinton
addressed the following letter to General
Washington, dated New York, September
26, 1780:—

" Sir,

Being informed that the King's adjutant-
general in America has been stopped under
Major-General Arnold's passports, and is
detained a prisoner in your excellency's
army, I have the honour to inform you, Sir,
I permitted Major Andre to go to Major-
General Arnold, at the particular request of
that general officer.   You will perceive,
Sir, by the inclosed paper*, that a flag of

* N. B. This was General Arnold's letter above
recited.

truce was sent to receive Major Andre, and passports granted for his return. I therefore cannot have a doubt but your excellency will immediately direct, that this officer has permission to return to my orders at New York.

" I have the honour to be,

your excellency's most obedient

and most humble servant,

" *His Excellency*   H, CLINTON."
General Washington."

This letter was not answered by General Washington before the 30th of September, 1780, during which time, from the date of Sir Henry Clinton's letter, and General Washington's answer, the board of general officers were sitting in judgment upon Major Andre's case, as referred to them by Washington; and a number of letters was sent by Sir Henry Clinton and General Robertson; one of which, from the latter, as

It is explanatory of General Greene's conduct, and shews the determined system he
meant to pursue after this silence, I think
necessary to insert it.   It is dated from the
Greyhound schooner, flag of truce, Dobbs's
Ferry, Oct. 2, 1780.   It also shews that
the friends of Major Andre were incessant
in their endeavours to rescue him from his
impending fate.   The letter is addressed to
General Washington :

" SIR,

" A note I have from General Greene
leaves me in doubt if his memory had served
him to relate with exactness the substance
of the conversation, that had passed between
him and myself, on the subject of Major
Andre.   On an affair of so much consequence to my friend, to the two armies, and
humanity, I would leave no possibility of a
misunderstanding,   and therefore take the
liberty to put in writing the substance of

M

what I said to General Greene. I offered to prove by the evidence of Colonel Robinson, and the officers of the Vulture, that Major Andre went on shore at General Arnold's desire, in a boat sent for him in a flag of truce; that he not only came on shore with the knowledge, and under the protection of the general who commanded in the district, but that he took no step while on shore, but by the direction of General Arnold, as will appear from the inclosed letter from him to your excellency. Under these circumstances I could not, and hoped you would not, consider Major Andre as a spy, for any improper phrase in his letter to you.

" The facts he relates correspond with the evidence I offer; but he admits a conclusion that does not follow. The change of clothes was ordered by General Arnold, under whose direction he necessarily was, while within his command.

" As General Greene and I did not agree in opinion, I wished that disinterested gen-tlemen, of knowledge of the laws of war and nations, might be asked their opinion on the subject, and mentioned Monsieur Knyp-hausen and General Rochambeau.

" I related that a captain had been deli-vered to Sir Henry Clinton as a spy, and he undoubtedly was such, but that it being sig-nified to him that you was desirous the man should be exchanged, he ordered him to be exchanged.

" I wished that an intercourse of such ci-vilities, as the rules of war admit of, might take off many of its horrors. I admitted that Major Andre had a great share of Sir Henry Clinton's esteem, and that he would be infinitely obliged by his liberation, and that, if he was permitted to return with me,

M 2

I would engage to have any person you would be pleased to name set at liberty.

" I added, that Sir Henry Clinton had never put to death any person for a breach of the rules of war, though he had, and now has, many in his power. Under the present circumstances, much good may arise from humanity ; much ill from the want of it, if that could give any weight. I beg leave to add, that your favourable treatment of Major Andre would be a favour I should ever be intent to return to any you hold dear.

" My memory does not retain with the exactness I could wish, the words of the letter which General Greene shewed me, from Major Andre to your excellency : for Sir Henry Clinton's satisfaction, I beg you will order a copy of it to be sent to me at New York.

" I have the honour to be your excellency's most obedient and most humble
servant,

" *His Excellency*   J. ROBERTSON."
General Washington."

Notwithstanding this pathetic and affecting letter, to which no answer was given,
because, through the still glowing and persecuting enmity of General Greene, it was
delivered too late, the sentence of the board
of general officers remained unreversed.

Major Andre, understanding that his fate
was finally determined on, and being informed
of the mode of his death, addressed the letter to General Washington which I have
already inserted*

This letter, however, was not answered :

* Vide Page 126.

but General Washington consulted the board
of officers on the subject.   Overcome with
remorse and sorrow, mingled with esteem,
they were all for granting this last request,
until General Greene insisted that his crime
was that of a common spy, and that the service and good of the American cause required the most exemplary punishment.
This he urged with such vehemence as induced a compliance in the rest; for, said he,
if he is shot, mankind will think there are
circumstances in his case, which intitled
him to notice and indulgence.

At length the awful period arrived; and
on the morning of the 2d of October, this
unhappy victim of the errors of others, was
led out to the place of execution.   As he
passed along, the American army were astonished at the dignity of his deportment, and
the manly firmness, and complacency of
countenance, which spoke the serene com-

posure of his mind; a glow of sympathy pervaded the breast of the soldiers, and the tears
of sensibility were visible in every eye. He
bowed himself, with a smile, to all he knew
in his confinement. When he approached
the fatal spot, and beheld the preparations,
he stopped, and paused, as if absorbed in
reflection; then quickly turning to the officer next him, he said—" What! must I die
in this manner?" Being told it was so ordered, he instantly said, " I am reconciled,
and submit to my fate, but deplore the
mode;—it will be but a momentary pang;"
and with a calmness that, while it excited
the admiration, melted the heart of every
spectator, performed the last offices to himself. He then requested that all around
him would bear witness to the world,—
" THAT HE DIED LIKE A BRAVE MAN!"
He perished universally esteemed and lamented; indeed, a general sorrow at his

fate pervaded all ranks of people through the continent of America.

As he passed the church where I was confined, while under trial, he asked the meaning of the crowd around it? and when told I was then upon my trial as an accomplice, he sighed, and said—" Poor man! *he knew nothing of the real business.*"

General Washington, in a letter to a friend, soon after the Major's execution, thus expresses himself:—

" Andre has met his fate, and with that fortitude which was expected from an accomplished man and a gallant officer; but I am mistaken if Arnold is not undergoing at this time the torments of a mental hell."

Even Major Andre's enemies, if it were

possible so amiable a character could have any, were as high in his applause, as the general mass were terrible in their execrations against General Arnold.

I cannot here omit some notice of the character given of Andre by Bushrod Washington, in the life of his relative, the general; for, as coming from an enemy, it ought to have a double effect to stamp the excellencies of the accomplished sufferer :—

" It would seem that art had been successfully employed in the embellishment of those fascinating qualities that nature had lavished on him. Possessed of a fine person and an excellent understanding, he had united the polish of a court, and the refinements given by education, to the heroism of a soldier. When youth, adorned with such rare accomplishments, is consigned prematurely to the grave, all our sensibilities

are roused, and for a moment human society
seems to sustain a deprivation by the melancholy stroke."

Colonel Hamilton, who was aid-de-camp
to General Washington, as I have already
mentioned, and the same that was killed in
a duel by Colonel Burr, vice-president of
the United States, whose name has been so
often mentioned in the public papers, and
who was lately tried for treason by order of
President Jefferson, in a letter written at
that time, says—

" There was something singularly interesting in the character and fortunes of Andre. To an excellent understanding, well
improved by education and travel, he united
a peculiar elegance of mind and manners,
and the advantage of a pleasing person.   It
is said he possessed a pretty taste for the fine
arts, and had himself obtained some profici-

ency in poetry, music, and painting. His
knowledge appeared without ostentation;
his sentiments were elevated, and inspired
esteem, as they had a softness that concili-
ated affection. His elocution was handsome; his address easy, polite and insinuating.

" By his merit he had acquired the unlimited confidence of his general, and was
making rapid progress in military rank and
reputation ; but, in the height of his career,
flushed with new hopes from the execution
of a project the most beneficial to his party
that could be devised, he is, at once, pre-
cipitated from the summit of prosperity,
and sees all the expectations of his ambition blasted, and himself ruined.

" The character I have given of him is
drawn partly from what I saw of him myself, and partly from the best information.

I am aware that a man of real merit is never
seen in so true a light, as through the medium of adversity;—the clouds that surround him, are as so many shades, that set
off his good qualities; misfortune cuts down
little vanities that, in prosperous times,
serve as so many spots in his virtues, and
give a tone to humanity that makes his
worth more amiable. His spectators, who
enjoy a happier lot, are less prone to detract
from it through envy, and are much disposed, through compassion, to give him the
credit he deserves, and, perhaps, to mag-
nify it."

Bushrod Washington, in his life of the
general, goes on to say :—

" The general-officers lamented the sentence, which the usages of war compelled
them to pronounce ; and, perhaps, on no
occasion of his life, did the commander in

chief obey with more reluctance the stern
mandates of duty and of policy: the sympathy excited among the American officers
was as universal as it is unusual on such occasions; and proclaims alike the merit of
him who suffered, and the humanity of
those who countenanced the punishment."

If we trace the history of military heroism
as far back as the annals of imperial Rome,
or that of Britain in any stage of its highest
glory, we cannot find a superior constella-
tion of admirable virtues in any man, not
even in the Mountjoys, Veres, and Cecils.
Major Andre testified that an English officer
never forgets what he owes to his country
in every clime; the wreaths that adorned
the brows of the Talbots, Salisburys, Mow-
brays, and a hundred other illustrious names
of former ages, were acquired by British
valour in British officers; nor have the Edwards and Henrys who have swayed the

British sceptre, disdained the duties of sub-
ordinate rank; for example, Henry the
Fifth in the glorious battle of Agincourt—
and Edward the Third acquired, in the hostile field, those laurels that adorned him as
an officer, and graced him as a monarch—
and Major Andre, in the sacrifice he
made of his life in the service of his sovereign, far surpassed the brave Greek, who
exclaimed—" What toils do I undergo, O
Athenians! that I may merit your approbation."

It was the courage, the virtue, and the
generous contempt of ease, wealth, and
danger, that gave English officers, in the
days of Queen Elizabeth, the highest lustre
in the eyes of Europe and their countrymen:
a distinction, that neither birth nor titles
can bestow; while the public approbation
was not confined to the barren praise of
fame, but more often productive of durable

emolument; and it is the glory of some of the noblest families in England, that merit in the field was rewarded by beauty at the court; and both have concurred to transmit their distinguished honours to posterity with undiminished lustre.

The guardian and protector of the rights of Europe, the restorer of British liberty, King William the Third, was indebted not only for his throne, but his glory, to the virtue and courage of British officers; and where they commanded he was never betrayed or disappointed.

The same spirit exhibited itself in a more splendid and glorious manner in the reign of Queen Anne—Churchill, Duke of Marlborough, still lives unrivalled in history; and need we go farther than the present day, when the glorious achievements of the im-

mortal Nelson still animate each British
breast?

A grateful nation will cherish the memory
of the brave; and our gracious sovereign,
the brightest ornament of whose reign has
been to reward distinguished merit, has
caused a monument to be erecte in Westminster Abbey, which, with the historic page
both of England and America, will perpe-
tuate the virtue and gallantry of Major Andre
through ages yet unknown.

*Description of the Monument in Westminster
Abbey, for* MAJOR JOHN ANDRE,
*designed by Robert Adam, Esq. Architect,
and executed in statuary Marble by Mr.
P. M. Van Gelder.*

This monument is composed of a sarcophagus, elevated on a pedestal, upon the

SACRED to the MEMORY
of
MAJOR JOHN ANDRÉ
&c. &c. &c.

Rob.ᵗ Adams Arch.ᵗ _ P.M.V. Gelder sculp.   Shirt sculpsit.

London. Published by Mathews & Leigh 1808.

pannel of which is engraved the following
inscription :—

SACRED TO THE MEMORY

of

MAJOR JOHN ANDRE,

Who, raised by his Merit, at an early Period

of his Life, to the Rank of

ADJUTANT-GENERAL OF THE BRITISH FORCES

IN AMERICA,

and, employed in an important but hazardous Enterprise,

FELL A SACRIFICE

to his

Zeal for his King and Country,

on the 2d of October, 1780, aged 29,

universally beloved and esteemed by the Army

in which he served, and lamented even

by his Foes.

His gracious Sovereign

KING GEORGE III.

has caused this Monument to be erected.

On the front of the sarcophagus, General
Washington is represented in his tent, at
the moment when he had received the report
of the court-martial held on Major Andre ;

N

at the same time a flag of truce arrived from
the British army, with a letter for General
Washington to treat for the Major's life.
But the fatal sentence being already passed,
the flag was sent back without the hoped
for clemency in his favour.

Major Andre received his condemnation
with that fortitude and resolution which had
always marked his character, and is represented going with unshaken spirit to meet
his doom.

On the top of the sarcophagus, a figure
of Britannia reclined, laments the premature
fate of so gallant an officer. The British
Lion too, seems instinctively to mourn his
untimely death.

Ancient nor modern history does not exhibit an instance, where an officer fell
so universally lamented by adversaries and

friends; an irrefragable proof of unsullied honour, and superior merit.

Eulogy cannot do sufficient justice to the deserts of this rarely-accomplished hero; and it must be some consolation to his surviving friends, that his and their foes drop the tear of sympathy, and mingle their sorrows at the same shrine, made sacred to virtue and truth.

Never can my memory cease to record the impassioned language of his countenance, and the energy with which he expressed his wish to be on board the Vulture, when viewing that ship from an upper window of my house; I knew not his inestimable merits: General Arnold, when he took my coat, said he was a young merchant, and from folly or pride had borrowed a British officer's coat from his acquaintance. No man's worth can be appreciated in the compass of a few

hours; my feelings were much exercised at
Major Andre's distress, so strongly depic-
tured in his countenance; I thought he
could have been returned, by a flag from
General Arnold, by any of the officers at
Stony Point, who were at that time under
his immediate command; and he was him-
sslf on the spot, on his way to West Point.
The arrangement for his return by land was
made between them the morning after Major
Andre came on shore, when I was confined
to my bed with the ague; and surely it was
more consistent with propriety to employ a
military man than a citizen; when there was
no impediment or contending influence to
have prevented General Arnold's placing
Major Andre in a state of perfect safety in
half an hour.   There appears to have been a
fatal infatuation throughout the whole of this
transaction.

The original interview was to have been

held between General Arnold and Major
Andre at Dobbs's ferry, on the east side of
the river; the Vulture had been stationed
there for the purpose some time previous to
her moving up to Haverstraw Bay. General Arnold had made several attempts to
go on board himself; on two occasions he
was near the ship, and was fired upon by
her, and the barge that conveyed him narrowly escaped the shot; this he declared to
me on his return from one of these excursions. Being disappointed, however, on
this account, the meditated interview was
proposed to take place in another way. The
letter from Major Andre, of the 7th Sept.
1780, to Colonel Sheldon, before recited,
and which was laid before the board of general-officers, states, that there had been a
correspondence between General Arnold
and Major Andre, under the signatures of
Gustavus and Anderson; and Colonel Sheldon, who had not heard of Anderson before,

when he inclosed this letter, is informed by
General Arnold, in his answer, that he expected a person by that name to come from
New York, for the purpose of bringing him
intelligence.   These letters were found
among General Arnold's papers, after his
flight from Robinson's house.   General Arnold explains this business fully in his letter
to General Washington, dated from New
York, Oct. 1, 1780, an extract of which I
here insert:—

" From your excellency's letter to Sir
Henry Clinton, I find a board of general-
officers have given it as their opinion, that
Major Andre comes under the description
of a spy ; my good opinion of the candour
and justice of those gentlemen leads me to
believe, that if they had been fully acquainted with every circumstance respecting
Major Andre, they would by no means have
considered him in the light of a spy, or even

of a prisoner. In justice to him I think it my duty to declare, that he came from on board the Vulture, at my particular request, by a flag sent on purpose for him by Joshua Smith, Esq. who had permission to go to Dobbs's ferry to carry letters, and for other purposes not mentioned, and to return; Mr. Smith, at the same time, had my private directions to go on board the Vulture, and bring on shore Colonel Robinson, or Mr. John Anderson, which was the name I had requested Major Andre to assume; at the same time I desired Mr. Smith to inform him, that he should have my protection, and a safe passport to return in the same boat, as soon as our business was completed. As several accidents intervened to prevent his being sent on board, I gave him my passport to return by land. Major Andre came on shore in his uniform, (without disguise,) which, with much reluctance, at my particular and pressing instance, he exchanged for another coat. I furnished him with a horse and saddle, and pointed out the rout by which he was to return; and, as commanding officer in the department, I had an undoubted right to transact all these matters, which, if wrong, Major Andre ought by no means to suffer for them."

From the above letter, as my name was confidentially mentioned by General Arnold, it would appear that I must have had some knowledge of the nature and extent of the objects meditated in this transaction, which, with the circumstance of lending my coat, were, with other collateral proofs, the strongest presumptions offered against me on my trial; on that account I was the more hardly pressed; yet General Arnold, in a postscript to a letter he addressed to General Washington, from on board the Vulture, the 25th of September, 1780, declares as follows:—

"N. B. In justice to the gentlemen of my family, Colonel Varick, and Major Franks,

I think myself in honour bound to declare,
that they, as well as Joshua Smith, Esq.
(who I know is suspected,) are totally ignorant of any transactions of mine, that they
had reason to believe were injurious to the
public."

Of this I shall take notice when I come to
my defence.

Major Andre's remains were interred in
an open field, belonging to a Mr. Mabie, in
the vicinity.

The Greyhound schooner, flag of truce,
which brought General Robertson's last letter to General Washington, dated on board
the schooner on the 2d of October, the day
Major Andre suffered, carried to New York
the melancholy account of that event.

No language can describe the mingled sen-

sations of horror, grief, sympathy, and revenge, that agitated the whole garrison; a
silent gloom overspread the general countenance; the whole royal army, and citizens
of the first distinction, went into mourning. Sir Henry Clinton, (although stung
with the deepest sorrow for the loss of so
valuable an officer,) who best knew how to
appreciate his merits, yet could not indulge
that spirit of resentment, in exercising the
dictates of passion or policy, by a retaliation
on a number of Carolina prisoners, of the
first distinction, who had forfeited their lives
agreeable to the usage of war. In almost
every instance, where humanity could be
exercised, the lenity of Sir Henry Clinton
was eminently conspicuous, both in civil
and in military matters. I cannot forbear to
mention a circumstance that occurred at
New York, while under his command. :—

A man, on the island of New York, who

had cultivated a garden with great care and labour, finding that it was constantly robbed at night, either by citizens or soldiers, was determined to terrify the thief. Accordingly, when dusk, he placed himself under the shelter of some bushes ;—he saw a man cross his fence, and in the very act of taking his property, when he immediately fired a gun, without ball or shot, to drive him away; this not having the desired effect, as he con-tinued his depredations, he immediately dis-charged another musket, well loaded, and shot him dead on the spot. The alarm brought the neighbours together, and the man surrendered himself into the hands of justice. There being no courts erected for criminal causes, Sir Henry Clinton ordered that, as the malefactor was rich, he should pay a heavy fine to the relations of the de-ceased, who were poor: the general thought it a better compensation than to take away the man's life.

There are many instances which I could
mention, of the benignity of Sir Henry
Clinton; but the case of a Captain Robinson, who was proved to be a spy, and several others, all of whom were released at the
desire of General Washington, shew that it
was the invariable system of Sir Henry
Clinton to prevent as much as possible the
horrors of war.

The solemn tragedy of the unfortunate
Major Andre being closed, I shall proceed
to relate what occurred on my own trial,
and the various hardships I encountered
through this unhappy transaction: I shall
also add such other matters of fact, as will
tend to throw light on the objects of this
publication.

It is worthy of remark, that Major Andre's awful fate did not in the least seem to
abate the fury of my persecution by General

Washington. Notwithstanding the declarations of both Arnold and Andre, my
guards were doubled, I was more closely
watched, and I was assured daily that, from
the additional evidences that were to be produced against me, I ought to prepare for the
same fate as had befallen Major Andre.

No farther testimony was, however, offered at Tappan, or Orange Town; for the
day after the sacrifice of Major Andre, the
3d of October, the American army broke
up their encampment, and marched to Piramus; whether from an apprehension of
being too near the British army, at that
place no more than 20 miles, or that the
country was sufficiently exhausted, I cannot pretend to determine; the former, however, was the general opinion, from the enraged state of the royal troops. I was
marched under the provost guard, on foot,
very weak and languid, although my horse

was ready to convey me, with one of my
servants to attend me; but he was not permitted to go, and the horse was stolen that
night. I was at first placed in a barn, with
my guard, but the night being wet and cold,
I was, through the intreaty of a Colonel
Lutterlough, a perfect stranger, suffered to
sit before the fire, in a good kitchen, attended by some of the guard.

During the night, being in much pain,
arising from the fever and ague, which had
not left me since my first arrest, one of the
guard appeared to sympathise very sincerely
with me, and, in a whisper, offered to aid
me in effecting my escape, if I found myself
able to undertake the fatigue, towards the
morning; being in no disposition of mind
or body to accept the offer, and fearing it a
trap to deceive me, I declined the solicitation, and had reason afterwards to find my
apprehensions true, for the fellow confessed

to a person of strict veracity, that he was employed to lay the temptation in my way.

At Piramus were a number of genteel families, who had taken refuge there from New York, and who, knowing myself and connections, earnestly importuned General Washington to permit their sending me some provisions; the same application was made at Tappan, by the family where the general resided, but the humane individuals received, at both places, a rude and an unfeeling denial.

The army did not long continue here, but proceeded to a place called Totowa Bridge, near the celebrated Falls of Pissaick. On the road I had another offer from two of my guard, that if I would make the attempt to escape at night, finding me better in health and spirits than I had been on the line of march, they would give me every assistance. Being natives of that part of the country, they assured me that I should be sheltered by their friends, who, they asserted, were attached to the King's interest. These people, I believe, were sincere; and I knew that the far greater part of the inhabitants in the vicinity were loyalists, and had taken the oath of allegiance to the king in the autumn of 1776: having, however, suffered so much already, and knowing that no evidence could touch my life, unless by subornation, I was unwilling to incur any risks, and therefore declined their offer.

It was near this place that Colonel Baylor, of the Virginia cavalry, was surprised, and the greater part of his troops either cut to pieces, or taken prisoners. The inhabitants of this district, from their known attachment to the British interest, were accused of having piloted the royal troops to this attack, on account of their being plundered of their property by the soldiery under Colonel Baylor's command. About mid-way between Paramus and Passaick Falls, at this place, my guard was relieved and doubled. The second night after leaving Paramus, I was placed under a strong guard at a public house, near Totowa Bridge; before this I was kept in the open air, and forced to lie on the ground, which Lord Stirling observing, as he rode by, mentioned the ill usage to General Washington, and requested, as a family friend, that I might be sheltered; this indulgence he reluctantly consented to. I was well guarded at this house, having a captain with two centinels without, and one within the room of my confinement. I was left to subsist in the best way I could; but this was not diffi-cult, as I received supplies of cash from a source which I was then unacquainted with.

At length I was here again brought before

o

the court-martial, when the following witnesses were produced, viz. Colonel Lamb,
Mr. Jonathan Laurence, Major-General
Howe, Captains Gardner and Hutchins,
and Commodore Bowen, with several
others.

The general purport of their testimony
was little more than presumptive evidence,
except that of Colonel Lamb, who declared
that he was present at General Arnold's
table, when the subject of the flags was introduced in conversation; and he confirmed
what I have already related on that
subject.

Through the indisposition of one of the
members of the court-martial, their sitting
was postponed for several days. This circumstance, with the comfort of having a bed
to rest on, and the privilege of procuring in
the interim my own food, gave me fresh

spirits to encounter the hardships of my situation.

On the recovery of the member who was indisposed, the court-martial sat every day for about a fortnight, but proceeded very slow in the examination of their witnesses; it was conjectured by my friends that the delay was occasioned by the hope that some new matter of evidence would have arisen; and no efforts were wanting on the part of the prosecutor to bring all the testimony against me which he could procure.

During this period, I received a very con-solatory message from my brother, the chief justice; my wife and family were permitted to see me, but not without some hesitation on the part of General Washington, who even reprehended Major-General Howe for his polite attention to them; the general, however, answered, that as she was a lady of his acquaintance, and a native of Carolina, no power on earth should prevent him from discharging those duties, which humanity and politeness demanded. An elder brother of mine, in the profession of the law, was ordered from camp, until the court-martial had gone through their evidence.

The examination of witnesses was protracted to a fortnight after my detention at Totowa Bridge; and no farther evidence appearing, I was allowed to call such as might assist in my defence, while a short time was allowed for me to draw it up.

As my life was at stake, and the interests of all that were dear to me were involved in my fate, my family then consisting of a tender wife and two young children, my energies were exerted to the utmost, and in the space of forty-eight hours I presented a defence to the court-martial, which filled a

quire of paper, closely written; I read it to
them, and a large part of the army, in the
presence of a great concourse of the inhabitants. I should have no objection to present it to the public, but on considering the
superior importance of the other parts of the
narrative, I have no doubt that the reader
will prefer its being dispensed with. On
delivering the papers to the judge-advocate
I was ordered to withdraw.

The defence principally consisted in comments upon the judicial power before whom
I was made amenable. The resolve of Congress which authorised my detention, was
passed on the 27th of February, 1778; it
states as follows,—" that whatever inhabi-
tant of these states shall kill, or seize, or
take, any loyal citizen or citizens thereof,
and convey him or them to any place within
the power of the enemy, or shall enter into
any combination for such purpose, or at-

tempt to carry the same into execution, or
hath assisted, or shall assist therein; or
shall, by giving intelligence, acting as a
guide, or in any other manner whatever, aid
the enemy in the perpetration thereof, he
shall suffer death by the judgment of a court-
martial, as a traitor, assassin, or spy, if the
offence be committed within seventy miles
of the head-quarters of the grand or other
armies of these states where a general officer
commands."

I contended that this mere resolve of congress could not abolish a fundamental principle established in any of the civil constitutions of states in the union; that the exercise of the power vested by this resolution,
deprived the subject of the right of trial by
jury, the great bulwark of individual freedom; and that it was in direct contradiction
to the declaration of the reasons which Con-

gress assign for their separation from the
power of Great Britain.

I shewed from several counter-resolutions
and solemn acts of congress, that this resolve was suited to the then special occasion, and was not meant to obtain a general
influence, but was only at that time applicable to Pennsylvania, the British troops
being in the possession of the capital of
Philadelphia.

And here it will not be inappropriate to
mention the sentiments of Dr. Gordon,
who, in a letter to his friend, on the subject of the American revolution, after reciting the resolution, says, " This resolution has been introduced to shew you what
a stretch of power congress have been guilty
of: they have hereby suspended, in particular cases, the judicial authority of the
Massachuset's state, which is not the seat

of war, and subjected certain criminals to a
trial by court-martial, instead of leaving
them to the laws of the state."—He goes
on to exemplify as follows: " At Providence a general-officer commands a small
army at the distance of forty-five miles from
Boston."—The Doctor proceeds most justly
to observe: " All bodies of fallible men
possessed of, or claiming power, ought to
be narrowly watched, or, from good or bad
intentions, they will transgress the limits of
their constitution, without a real necessity."
This letter, reciting the resolve of congress,
was dated from Boxbury, June 1, 1778.

It must appear strange to the world, that
Congress should violate those rights of citi-
zenship, for which their country was drenched
in blood. THIS FLAGRANT INJUSTICE
WILL MARK THE SAVAGE FEROCITY WITH
WHICH THEIR GENERAL SOUGHT MY
LIFE, (not sufficiently glutted with that

of the accomplished Andre,) *and ought to be a warning to posterity how they invest tyrants with any sort of power, that they can with impunity abuse.*

Without any one as my counsel I was compelled to enter on my defence, which I did with the more cheerfulness, from the candid and impartial manner in which the trial was conducted by the judge-advocate, and the court-martial in general, but more particularly the president, Colonel Henry Jackson, of the town of Boston, in the Massachuset's State.

In order to form a correct idea of the reasoning offered in my defence, it will be necessary here to repeat the charge, to shew the artful manner in which it was drawn up by the prosecutor, *General Washington himself:*

" You stand charged for aiding and assisting Benedict Arnold, late a major-general in

our service, in a combination with the enemy,
for the purpose of taking, seizing, and
killing such of the loyal citizens and soldiers
as were in garrison at West Point and its
dependencies."

I insisted, in my answer, upon the following general principles :—

1st. That General Arnold was actually
a major-general in the American service at
the very time I was engaged in the combination specified in the charge, and that I
could not have had any agency without his
sanction and direction ; for General Arnold
did not relinquish his commission until the
1st of October, 1780, the day previous to
Major Andre's death, as will appear from
his following letter to General Washington,
when at New York:

" Sir,

" I take this opportunity to inform your

excellency, that I consider myself no longer
acting under the commission of Congress,
their last to me being among my papers at
West Point; you, Sir, will make such use
of it as you think proper.

" At the same time I beg leave to assure
your excellency, that my attachment *to the
true interests of my country is invariable*, and
that I am actuated by the same principle
which has ever been the governing rule of
my conduct in this unhappy contest.

" I have the honour to be, &c.

B. ARNOLD."

The testimony of the two Colquhouns
proved that General Arnold himself gave the
instructions for us to go on board the Vulture; that he furnished the boat, directed
the muffling the oars, offered the reward for
their labour, and, in case of non-compliance,

threatened the punishment he was authorised
to inflict.

2dly. That the charge, in the present instance, was a charge of treason against the
United States ; treason being a crime of the
highest magnitude known in the law, the
law demanded that it should be supported
by the strongest testimony.

Under this head I proved that the constitution of the State of New York had confirmed all the acts of parliament, that had
been in use by the colony of New York
under the ancient government, previous to
the declaration of independence in July,
1776, and, consequently, the act of parliament respecting treason, passed in the reign
of Edward the Third, as it had heretofore
been used and considered, was in full force,
and applicable to the case in question.

This statute enacts, that each and every separate overt-act of treason shall be supported by the testimony of two witnesses, agreeably to the sacred scriptures, " By the mouth of two witnesses every word shall be established."

In contradiction of this statute, I proved that the whole of the evidence that had been offered, could amount to no more than presumptive evidence.

3dly. I urged as an established maxim, that in every charge or indictment for high crimes or misdemeanors, the knowledge of the party, charged with having committed the criminality, should be so stated in the charge or indictment, and made out by the most clear and conclusive testimony.

I demonstrated, from the particulars in the charge, that this was not the case, and that not one of the witnesses had suggested the idea; not even Colonel Hamilton, who attempted it by some artful reasonings upon what I had said in my examination before General Washington, on my being first brought before him. Colonel Harrison declared, that I delivered my declaration to General Washington with firmness and perspicuity, and was unembarrassed until informed by the general, that Arnold had fled to the British standard; I then appeared, for a moment, astonished, it being the first intimation I had received of his flight. At that time I could scarcely believe General Washington's assertion, and frankly told him, that if there was any error or mismanagement, he must look to General Arnold, I having acted solely by his direction, and had uniformly done what I conceived to be for the best interest of America.

4thly. I averred, that in all courts of jus-

tice in particular, every man, however accused, was always presumed innocent until
he was proved guilty; and that the most
wise and rigid administrators of justice upon
the bench, and otherwise, had invariably
determined, that where the cause was
doubtful, the scale of justice should prepon-
derate in favour of the accused, upon the
principle already established,—that it was
better that ninety-nine criminals should pass
unpunished, than that one innocent man
should unjustly suffer.

5thly I proved, from the authority and
usage of all courts of justice, that where the
party's declaration or confession is brought
as evidence against himself, that the whole
must be taken together, and not abstract-
edly; as, if otherwise, through the art of the
accuser, the most innocent man might be
made to contradict and condemn himself;
and—

6thly. And lastly, I corroborated these general principles by authorities founded in reason and in law ; and the concurrent usage of civil policy in all Christian and enlightened nations.

After establishing these positions, I entered upon a critical examination of the whole evidence that had been offered, and clearly proved, that not one of the positions supported the charge exhibited against me, upon the slightest grounds of reason or equity.

I noticed many contradictions in the testimony of the Marquis de la Fayette, and the evidence of General Knox, as well as that of Colonels Harrison and Hamilton, and made particular remarks on the reasonings of the latter, who, as a minion of the prosecutor, appeared very desirous to prove me guilty.

As these were the principal evidences, and the whole of what was adduced on the part of the prosecution, of any material consequence, and these too merely of a circumstantial nature, I informed the court I might now safely rest on my defence.

But, lest any misconception should arise in a case wherein I was so deeply interested I recapitulated the whole evidence,—with this solemn appeal—That what I had declared to General Washington was strictly true—what I had mentioned to my confidential friend, Colonel Hay—what I then declared to the court-martial—what I should continue to declare, through every period of my life—and in that solemn day, when an omniscient God should scrutinise my conduct!

Having finished my defence, I was remanded under guard, and conveyed to the

P

place of my confinement. Previous to my arrival, some person had mentioned to the
woman of the house, in which I was impri-
soned, that I was *condemned* by the court-
martial, on which the good housewife, in a
furious rage, refused me admittance. The
reader may conceive that I was not a little
shocked with this instance of vulgar un-
feelingness ; another place was therefore
found for my reception, in which I waited
in suspense for several days, but consoled
myself with the reflection that I had discharged my duty, to the extent of my abi-
lity, for the benefit of my distressed family ;
and composed my mind to support with resignation and fortitude whatever might befal
me.

During this confinement, I had a visit
from two of the court-martial, (a Major and
a Captain,) accompanied by the Judge-Advocate : the court-martial consisted of a Co-

lonel, Major, and twelve Captains, principally collected from the Connecticut line of
the army, who, being General Arnold's
countrymen, it was supposed, would be
more enraged against me, if it had been
proved that I was in his confederacy; and I
must confess that, at the time, I considered
them in no other light than a *packed* jury:
but no gentlemen could have acted with
more candour and liberality, after the principal evidences were taken.

The object of the Major's interview was
to obtain from me an explanation of the reason why my name was inserted amongst
those of the inhabitants, that were found
upon Major Andre? This appeared to be a
great stumbling-block to him, and which,
as I have already observed, I could not remove; he left me, apparently much affected
by my unhappy situation, and said, the

court-martial would soon determine on my case.

Some few days after, I had a visit from another of the court-martial, who, during the whole of my trial, sympathised much with me, and expressed himself greatly concerned, lest General Washington should direct a re-consideration of the sentence that had been passed.

Although these hints tended to re-animate my hopes, they were not satisfactory, for I knew the malevolence of the prosecutor against my family, and was convinced that after having gone such lengths illegally and unconstitutionally, he would not readily relinquish his revenge, while there was the least colour of justice to gratify it. I was informed that there were those about his person, who were inclined to cherish in his mind sentiments prejudicial to my hopes; and, among them, the infamous Colonel Bull, whose notorious character has already been exposed. I depended greatly upon the open and unreserved assertions of General Greene, the principal confidant of General Washington, who freely gave his opinion, that if I was guilty, there was not sufficient testimony against me to touch my life; and I knew also that my nephew, Colonel William Livingston, was unwearied in his solicitations with the general to interest him in my behalf, and to whom General Greene owed considerable obligations,

Thus languishing under the various impressions of hope and fear, I seriously wished a termination to an existence that had become a burthen to me;—my days were imbittered by the thoughts of my afflicted family.—Even at this distance of time, my heart recoils at the recollection of those

scenes of horror that tortured my imagination.
It was conjectured by some, that General
Washington had transmitted my case to congress for ultimate direction ; by others, that,
as I had appealed to the civil authority, he
applied to the executive power of the state
to which I belonged.   I was lost in conjecture,—when, on the morning of the 10th of
November, I was roused from my stupor by
an officer of the horse, who delivered a note
to the officer of the guard, under whose custody I was, and then, turning to me, desired
me to follow him immediately; I most cheerfully obeyed, for any situation was better
than the miserable state of suspense which
I had so long endured.

A troop of horse was recruiting at the
door, and a led horse was brought to
me, which I was commanded to mount.
When we were at some distance from the
house, I ventured to ask where we were

going ? The officer sternly replied, I should soon see. Tortowa bridge lies in a valley, and on reaching the summit of the eastern hill, I could perceive that he had taken a circuitous road towards the Hudson River. I now indulged myself with the hope that perhaps, I might once more, see my little family. We rode silently on, followed by our guides with drawn swords; various colourings of different impressions that stole across my mind, respecting my future des_tiny, perplexed me much; when I was roused from my reverie, by a stroke upon my horse, and a thundering oath that if I did not press on, we should not arrive at our journey's end that night. I endeavoured to hasten the poor emaciated animal, but my efforts were unavailing, till the humane officer dismounted, and gave me one of his spurs; with this aid, we soon reached the skirts of Paramus, where we halted to refresh ourselves and horses, at a Dutchman's tavern, for by that name almost all the inns are called; the landlord knew me, and was preparing to dress me a chicken, but my gruff companion swore in broken high-Dutch and English, that the peef and bork was good kanough for a damned dory. The landlord, however, soothed his choler, by offering him some cyder spirits, which instantly produced so wonderful an effect, that from a single draught, the swarthy gloom of his countenance assumed a milder aspect. Having dined, we instantly proceeded; my companion now became garrulous, and in his broken elocution, discovered that he was a Pennsylvanian soldier in the regiment of Young Losberg, who had deserted his colours. A few miles farther, we perceived the sign of a public house, and as I found the cyder spirit had so excellent an effect, I pressed him to take another libation to Bacchus, and to permit me to treat the troop, to which he

readily consented; but heavily did I re-
enter the house, for it was here that the
unfortunate Andre and myself had halted
when under the charge of Major Talmadge,
on our way to Tappan from West Point.
My German commander now became quite
fresh and lively, and disputed upon political subjects with the landlord, who told
him he only differed from a *hog*, for want
of bristles; to which my hero replied by
calling him a Dory tog, (meaning a *Tory
dog*,) and dat he was worser dan turncoad
Arnold. I supplied him abundantly with
the country nectar, which detained him
until near dark; I did this designedly,—as I
began to suspect it was his orders to convey
me to West Point; in which conjecture I
was not mistaken,—for when we had proceeded a few miles farther, he informed me
his orders were to that effect. My next plan
was to linger on the way as much as I possibly could, in order to make it late before

we could arrive at King's Ferry, in the hope
of continuing on the west side of the river,
and enjoying the happiness of seeing my
family, which were then at my brother's,
two miles and a half from the ferry, and
whose house we were obliged to pass.   In
this scheme I was materially aided by the
weariness of the poor beast on which I
rode ; and, from the double motive of pity
to him, and the much stronger one of delay-
ing our journey as much as possible, I made
it, notwithstanding my companion's entreaties, quite late before we reached my
brother's, at Haverstraw.   Here I met Colonel Burr, who was on a visit, and who, to
my inexpressible satisfaction, prevailed upon
my commander to halt for the night.   Most
of the family had retired to bed, but, upon
the unexpected news of my arrival, they
soon rose, and the happiness of again be-
holding the beloved object of my heart, at
once banished all my past sorrows.   But my

joy was momentary—for the officer of my
guard informed the family, he was ordered
to proceed with me to West Point with all
possible dispatch, and that whatever conversation we wished, must take place that
night, as he was compelled to separate us
by break of day. The better to secure me,
he slept on a sofa in the same room with
my family during the night, although Colonel Burr was my security, and carefully
posted the guards around the doors and
windows, giving them a countersign in case
of alarm.

This was a distressing scene to my poor
partner in sorrow, for though she bore her
affliction with an exemplary patience, yet
she was so overcome with this military parade as to be totally disqualified for much
conversation, nor had I any to impart but
of a nature too gloomy to afford her any
comfort.

The morning soon came, and with it a
heavy storm ; Colonel Burr endeavoured to
persuade the officer, from the weak and languid state I was in, to suffer me to remain
until the tempest was abated, which he consented to do, if Colonel Burr would ask permission from Colonel James Livingston, at
Verplank's Point, to whom I was to be sent.
A messenger was accordingly dispatched for
this purpose, who instantly returned with
a message, that the request could not be
granted, reprimanding the officer for his
delay.   Thus situated, I was compelled to
leave my family in the utmost anxiety of
mind.   Being arrived at the ferry, I was
placed in an open boat, and conveyed eighteen miles through a most violent storm,
to Robinson's house, the first scene of my
sorrow ; I was detained here only till the
storm abated, when I was sent across the
river to the place where I was first confined, but apparently under a stronger guard

than before attended me. Upon my arrival here, a suspicion forcibly occurred to
my mind, that as I was charged with con-
federating to deliver this post into the hands
of the British army, it might be General
Washington's design to execute the sentence
of the court-martial at that place, as more
exemplary to the garrison, from the crime
I was charged with having committed. I experienced many inconveniences in this place,
for as it was a garrison where there was no
market, I could obtain no provisions. I
therefore addressed a line to General Heath,
from Massachuset's, who commanded here,
and informed him that I was in a starving
condition : he immediately gave directions
to the commissary for rations, such as they
were, and by his aid-de-camp, a Major Ly-
man, he informed me, that I was at liberty
to write to my friends for whatever supplies
I might want, previously submitting my
letter to his inspection ; this I readily did,

and was soon furnished with the articles that were requisite.

Availing myself of this condescension on the part of General Heath, I wrote again to my friends, to supply me with clothing, bedding, and other necessaries, not attainable in the garrison; I took the liberty to express myself very freely on the severity of Colonel James Livingston's conduct, in sending me, when in a violent fever, through so severe a storm, a harshness which no policy could warrant, and which was even repugnant to humanity. After a day's detention of my letter, I was indulged with his answer to the following effect,—" that in my situation, language less spirited would be more becoming; and that it would be as improper for him to transmit my letter, as it was unbecoming in me to write it." Being so often, and continuing so long under the apprehension of death, " *per fas aut nefas.*"

I had lost all fears of that event, and as a
week had now elapsed, and my execution
was still suspended, I began to alter my first
opinion, and dismissed the apprehension
that I was sent here for that purpose. Although unfortunate, I was not abject; I
therefore wrote to the general a firm, decent,
yet animated letter, requesting to know the
cause of my being sent to West Point; informing him that, as a citizen, I had been
illegally tried by a court-martial, which had
reported my case to General Washington;
I also desired to know the determination of
that court-martial, if he was instructed or
allowed by General Washington to afford
me such information; inclosing at the same
time a printed copy of the constitution, to
justify the validity of my assertion.

Several days had now elapsed, and I had
some indulgences allowed, which I had
not heretofore received. This change in-

spired some hope of emancipation ; when, contrary to my expectation, on the 18th of November, I was desired by a Captain Sheppard, of the New Jersey Continental troop, to prepare in an hour's time to follow him ; and, within the time limited, he came, attended by his company, consisting of about fifty men. I marched with him, across the Highland Mountains, to a place called Smith's Clove, a valley, which took its name from my family, as possessing a greater part of the land it contained, as well as round its vicinity.

Captain Sheppard, perceiving the very infirm state to which I was reduced, when we arrived at the settlement, very humanely proposed, that if I could procure a horse, he would indulge me with riding ; but as this accommodation could not be obtained at that place, I expressed a wish to be permitted to pass three miles out of the main road, to a farm belonging to my family, where a brother of mine resided, as I had no doubt I should there succeed in procuring horses; to this he acceded; and mentioned, that the place of my destination was known only to the Sheriff of the County of Orange, at Goshen, about thirty miles from West Point.

The hospitality with which the captain and soldiers were treated on our arrival, and the unrestrained freedom they had taken with the strong cider of the country, threw them entirely off their guard, and the servant whom I had been allowed to have with me at West Point, having been dismissed, to return to my family at Haverstraw, had in his way passed on before me, and informed the tenants of the family estate of the situation in which I was placed; many of whom came to see me that night, and, in their zeal to serve me, were very solicitous that I

Q

should avail myself of the opportunity which
circumstances then presented me, to effect
my escape. This district was celebrated for
the attachment of the inhabitants in general
to the British interest, who had frequently
encouraged, and protected parties, from
New York, in their mountainous recesses;
and it was in this defile, that the celebrated
Captain Moody, in May, 1781, intercepted
an express from General Washington to congress, communicating the result of his interview with the commanders of the land and
naval forces of France, and which disclosed
to Sir Henry Clinton, the design of General
Washington to attack the seat of the British
power, New York; and enabled Sir Henry
to take the necessary precautions, to prevent
the combination, by strengthening the garrison; in withdrawing from Lord Cornwallis
a part of the troops, then under his command
at Williamsburg, in Virginia; and ordering
his lordship to repass James River, and

retire to Portsmouth, when possessed of every advantage. I make this digression, as the importance of the passes of the Highlands was, and possibly may be again, the subject of military contemplation. I must be allowed to add, that almost all the communications between Canada and New York passed through this place, there being a regular connection of the King's friends, where they could take their stages during the whole war, in the greatest safety.

But to return to the narrative.—The debilitated state of my health would not, had I been inclined, have permitted me to accept the many offers of assistance to effect my escape; nor could I have conceived myself honourably justified in adopting a measure of that kind, after the humane and liberal manner in which I had been used by Captain Sheppard, who not only mitigated the severity of my situation, by every amiable

act of sympathy the next day, on the road
to Goshen, by suffering me to ride there
unguarded the greater part of the way; but
when I arrived, and the sheriff, into whose
hands he had been directed to deliver my
mittimus, was preparing, in compliance
with its command, to place me in the most
safe and secure custody, he became my advocate, interceded in my behalf for a relax-
ation of his rigour, and declared the honourable manner in which I had regarded the
confidence he had placed in me on the
road.

The *mittimus*, under which I was committed, was signed by or William Williams, Gilbert Livingston, and Robert
Harper, stiling themselves a committee of
the commissioners for detecting conspiracies within the state of New York; this
was as arbitrary an act of oppressive tyranny,
and as unconstitutional, even upon their

own principles, as the military tribunal from which I appeared to be discharged.

A board of commissioners had been appointed, in the first stages of the war, for the purpose of detecting conspiracies; but after the constitution was framed, defining the liberties of the subject, and the legislature of the state had been convened, this board and all committees were abolished; being only tolerated until the regular government was organised. I was not in a situation, however, to resist this stretch of arbitrary power; and, not long after my new confinement, the grand jury of the county met in this place, it being the principal county town. Much art and industry were employed by the attorney-general, to induce the grand jury to find a bill of indictment against me; but the injustice and cruelty of attempting to place a man's life in danger twice for one and the same offence, was

spiritedly rejected by them; of this I was
informed by several members who composed
the grand jury, who reprobated the measure
as illegal, unconstitutional, and barbarous.
After this attempt, many who had been refused access to me, were now admitted;
my family were allowed to visit me, and to
administer those supplies, and consolations,
which the state of my health rendered indispensably necessary, from the length of my
confinement, and the vicissitudes I had
undergone.

A short time after this, the jail was filled
with those who professed themselves to be
the King's friends; Tories, and those who
were prisoners of war; felons, and characters of all colours and descriptions. This
occasioned a special commission of oyer and
terminer, or general jail delivery to be
issued. The wretched state of the country
operated only to increase its miseries, by

the infliction of new and unheard-of punish-
ments. At the session of that court, another
attempt was made with the grand jury, to
persuade them to find a bill of indictment,
but all their efforts were in vain; this grand
jury, as well as their predecessors, were
composed of the first people of the county,
attached to the ancient government, and
heartily wearied with the confusion and dis-
tractions of the unsettled state of public
affairs.

The campaign of this year was now over,
and never were congressional affairs in a more
ruinous state. The general disposition of
those who had been most active became
lukewarm, and the disaffected to the emancipation of the empire by the measure of independence daily increased, from a variety
of causes; and, among others, the introduc-
tion of French troops was not the least; for
the remembrance of their cruelties in the

Canadian war, was not obliterated from the
minds of the most intelligent observers, who
dreaded the re-possession of Canada by that
power : others, who were strenuous advocates of Independence, were driven to
greater exertions from the declaration of
the French monarch,—that the situation of
European affairs would require all the exertions which that nation could make, for its
own preservation ; and that all his strength
was necessary to maintain the common
cause, which might render America as much
service at home as elsewhere; and congress
was plainly informed, that after that campaign, they must expect from France no
farther pecuniary, or military assistance.
The address, also, of General Arnold to
the inhabitants of America, after having
abandoned the Republican cause, power-
fully influenced the minds of the citizens;
the facts it contained, in justification of his
conduct, were unanswerable; and, as it

operated to create peculiar vengeance against those who were the king's friends, it had a singular effect in exasperating the leaders of opposition, against myself under the impression of my being charged as connected with him, in the unhappy transaction wherein Major Andre fell a sacrifice.

For the sake of elucidation, I will here insert this address.

"*New York, Oct.* 7, 1780.

" I should forfeit, even in my own opinion, the place I have so long held in your's, if I could be indifferent to your approbation, and silent on the motives which induced me to join the King's army.

" A very few words however, shall suffice on a subject so personal; for to the thousands who suffer under the tyranny of the usurpers in the revolted provinces, as well as to the great multitude who have long wished for its subversion, this instance of my conduct can want no vindication ; and as to that class of men who are criminally protracting the war, from sinister views, at the expense of the public interest, I prefer their enmity to their applause. I am, there-fore, only concerned in this address, to ex-plain myself to such of my countrymen as want abilities or opportunities, to detect the artifices by which they are duped.

" Having fought by your side when the love of our country animated our arms, I shall expect from your justice and candour, what your deceivers with more art and less honesty, will find inconsistent with their views to admit.

" When I quitted domestic happiness for the perils of the field, I conceived the rights of my country in danger, and that duty and honour called me to her defence. A redress of grievances was my only object, and aim; however I acquiesced in a step which I thought precipitate; the acclamation of independence: to justify this measure, many plausible reasons were urged, which could no longer exist, when Great Britain, with the open arms of a parent, offered to embrace us as children, and grant the wished-for redress.

" And now that our worst enemies are in our bosom, I should change my principles if I conspired with their designs; yourselves being judges, was the war less just because our fellow subjects were our foes? You have felt the torture with which we have raised our arms against a brother.—God incline the guilty protractors of these unnatural dissensions to resign their ambition, and cease from their delusions in compassion to kindred blood.

" I anticipate your question, was not the war a defensive one, until the French joined in the combination? I answer that I thought so. You will add, was it not afterwards necessary till the separation of the British Empire was complete? By no means.—In contending for the welfare of my country, I am free to declare my opinion, that this end attained, all strife should have ceased.

" I lamented, therefore, the impolicy, tyranny, and injustice, which, with a sovereign contempt, the people of America, studiously neglected to take their collective sentiments on the British proposals of peace ; and to negociate, under a suspension of arms, for an adjustment of differences; I lamented it as a dangerous sacrifice of the great interests of this country, to the partial views of a proud, ancient, and crafty foe. I had my suspicions of some imperfections in

the councils, on proposals prior to the
commission of 1778, but having then less
to do in the cabinet than the field, (I will
not pronounce peremptorily as some may,
and perhaps justly, that congress have ex-
iled them from the public eye) I continued
to be guided in the negligent confidence of
a soldier. But the whole world saw, and
all America confessed, that the overtures
of the second commission, exceeded our
wishes, and expectations; and if there was
any suspicion of the national liberality, it
arose from its excess.

Do any believe that we were really at
that time, entangled by an alliance with
France? Unfortunate delusion! They have
been duped by a virtuous credulity, in the
incautious moments of intemperate passion,
to give up their felicity, to serve a nation
wanting both the will and power to protect
us; and aiming at the destruction both of

the mother country and the provinces. In
the plainness of common sense, for I pretend not to casuistry, did the pretended
treaty with the court of Versailles, amount
to more than an overture to America?
Certainly not: because no authority had
been given by the people to conclude it,
nor to this very hour have they authorised
its ratification. The articles of confirmation
remain still unsigned.

" In the firm persuasion therefore, that
the private judgment of an individual citizen of this country, is as free from all con-
ventional restraints since, as before, the
insidious offers of France, I preferred those
from Great Britain ; thinking it infinitely
wiser, and safer, to cast my confidence upon
her justice and generosity, than trust a mo-
narchy too feeble to establish your inde-
pendency, so perilous to her distant domi-
nions, the enemy of the protestant faith,

and fraudulently avowing an affection for
the liberties of mankind, while she holds
her native sons in vassalage and chains.

" I affect no disguise, and therefore frankly
declare, that in these principles, I had
determined to retain my arms and command,
for an opportunity to surrender them to
Great Britain; and in concerting the measures for a purpose in my opinion, as grateful, as it would have been beneficial to my
country, I was only solicitous to accomplish an event of decisive importance, and
to prevent as much as possible in the execution of it, the effusion of blood.

" With the highest satisfaction, I bear testimony to my old fellow soldiers, and citizens, that I find solid ground to rely upon
the clemency of our sovereign, and abun-
dant conviction, that it is the generous
intention of Great Britain, not only to leave

the rights and privileges, of the colonies
unimpaired, together with their perpetual
exemption from   taxation, but to super-
add such farther benefits as may consist
with the common prosperity of the empire;
in short, I fought for much less than the
parent country is willing to grant to her
colonies, or such as they can be able to
receive and enjoy.

"Some may think I continued in the strug-
gle of the unhappy days too long, and
others that I quitted it too soon.—To the
first I reply, that I did not see with their
eyes, nor perhaps had so favourable a situation to look from, and that by our common
master I am willing to stand or fall.   In
behalf of the candid among the latter, some
of whom I believe serve blindly, but ho-
nestly, in the band I have left, I pray God
to give them all the light requisite to
consult their own safety before it is too late :

and with respect to the herd of censurers, whos eenmity to me originates in their hatred to the principles by which I am now led to devote my life to the reunion of the British Empire, and as the best and only means to dry up the streams of misery that have deluged this country, they may be assured that conscious of the rectitude of my intentions, I shall treat their malice and calumnies with contempt and neglect.

B. ARNOLD.

Besides this address to the inhabitants at large, General Arnold issued a proclamation to his late brethren in arms, wherein he says " You are promised liberty, but is there an individual in the enjoyment of it, except your oppressors? Who among you dare speak, or write, what he thinks against the tyranny which has robbed you of your property, imprisons your persons, drags you forcibly to the field of battle, and is

R

daily deluging your country, with your
blood? You are flattered with indepen-
dance, as preferable to a redress of grievances;
and to obtain that shadow you forego substantial happiness, and involve yourselves
in all the wretchedness of poverty. The
rapacity of your own rulers has already rendered you incapable of supporting the pride
of character they taught you to aim at, and
must, inevitably, shortly belong to one or
other of these great powers which their
folly and wickedness have drawn into the
conflict. What is America now? a band of
widows, orphans, and beggars; and can
you, who have been soldiers in the continental army, can you, at this day want evidence that the funds of your country are
exhausted, or that the managers have applied them to their own private use? In
either case, you surely no longer continue in
this service with honour, and advantage;
you have hitherto been their supporters in

that cruelty, which, with an equal indiffe-
rence to yours, as well as to the labour and
blood of others, is devouring a nation that
from the moment you quit their colours,
will be redeemed from their tyranny.

The effect of the address and proclamation was various, They gave infinite satisfaction to the moderate, and those who were
the advocates for peace, in the reunion of
the empire, while they opened the eyes
of the uninformed; yet on the other hand,
they stimulated the advocates for independence, to the most violent exertion; and
those who were the unhappy victims of
their power, felt all the force and influence
of their vengeance. Many matters of the
most interesting nature, respecting the state
of public concerns, and congress, were
never, at any period of the war, involved in
such an entangled labyrinth of embarrass-
ments. Two parties agitated the congress,

the one adhered implicitly to the advice of
General Washington, the other party were
apprehensive of laying the foundation for a
standing army, which they considered de-
structive to the liberties of a free people,
and were unwilling to give a sanction to
its influence, by encreasing the military force
in the number already enlisted to serve during the war.

As with individuals, so political bodies,
and states, when their affairs fall to the
lowest ebb, they are either sunk into de-
spondency, or are roused to more vigorous
exertions; and there cannot be a more true
test of this observation in communities,
than when their public measures are stained
with a spirit of bitterness. Under the influence of this principle, the legislature of
the state of New York, passed an act con-
verting the testimony which was necessary
to convict in a charge of treason, to wit, by

two evidences, to each separate overt act :
and by another clause, made the testimony
in cases of felony sufficient to criminate in
treason ; and to suffer the act to operate as
well to the past, as all future treasons that
might be committed ; contrary to ancient
usage, and the established law of the land.
The established principles upon which the
Federal government acted in the constitution of general government of the United
States, are as follows : and these articles of
the constitution of America, were entered
into by a convention of only nine of the
states held at New York, and transmitted
for their approbation, by General Washington who was president of this convention,
and from which I shall make a few extracts.

ARTICLE I.

Section 9.—The privileges of the habeas
corpus shall not be suspended, unless

when in cases of rebellion, or invasion, the public safety may require it.

No bill of attainder or expost facto law shall be passed.

ARTICLE III.

Section 1.—The judicial power of the United States, shall be vested in one supreme court, and in such inferior courts, as the congress may from time to time ordain and establish. The judges both of the supreme and inferior courts, shall hold their offices during good behaviour, and shall at stated times receive for their services a compensation, which shall not be diminished during their continuance in office.

Section 2.—The judicial power shall extend to all cases in law, and equity, arising under this constitution, the laws of the United States and treaties

made, or which shall be made, under
their authority; to all cases affecting
ambassadors, other public ministers,
and consuls, to all cases of admiralty
maritime jurisdiction: to controversies
to which the United States may be a
party, to controversies between two
or more states, between a state and citizens of another state, between citizens of different states; between citizens of the same state claiming lands,
under grants of different states, or between a state or citizens thereof, and
foreign states, citizens or subjects.

In all cases affecting ambassadors, or
other public ministers and consuls, and
those in which a state shall be party,
the supreme court shall have original
jurisdiction.   In all the other cases before-mentioned, the supreme court shall
have appellate jurisdiction both as to

law, and fact, with such exceptions, and under such regulations, as congress shall make.

The trial of all crimes, except in cases of impeachment, shall be by jury; and such trial shall be held in the state, where the said crimes shall have been committed; but when not committed in any state, the trial shall be at such place or places as the congress may by law have directed.

Section 3.—Treason against the United States shall consist only in levying war against them, or in adhering to their enemies, giving them aid and comfort.

No person shall be convicted of treason unless on the testimony of two witnesses to the same overt act, or confession in open court.

The congress shall have power to declare the punishment of treason; but no at-

tainder of treason shall work corruption
of blood, or forfeiture, except during
the life of the person attainted.

ARTICLE IV.

Section 1.—Full faith and credit, shall
be given in each state to the public
acts, records, and judicial proceedings
of every other state; and the congress
may by general laws, prescribe the manner, in which such acts, records, and
preceedings, shall be proved, and the
effect thereof.

Section 2.—The citizens of each state
shall be entitled to all privileges and im-
munities of citizens in the several states.

A person charged in any state with treason, felony, or other crime, who shall
fly from justice, and shall be found in
another state, shall on demand of the
executive authority of the state from
which he fled, be delivered up, to be

removed to the state having jurisdiction of thecrime.

The congress shall have power to dispose and make all needful rules, and regulations, respecting the territory, or other property belonging to the United States; and nothing in this constitution, shall be so construed as to prejudice any claims of the United States, or of any particular state.

Done in convention by the unanimous consent of the states present, the seventeenth day of September, in the Year of our Lord one thousand seven hundred and eighty-seven, and of the Independence of the United States of America, the twelfth.

GEORGE WASHINGTON,
President.

I have taken the liberty of making the above extracts, as it plainly exhibits the in-

justice and asperity exercised on this occasion, against myself, and which was in
some instances practised on others ; an injustice so totally repugnant to the general
principles from which the opposition to
Great Britain first started, and to which they
returned, as appears in the above-recited
solemn acts, at the conclusion of the War.
That which was law and the rule of right
to-day, was renounced the succeeding, as
policy dictated the application to the party
interested on the occasion ; indeed it was
difficult to know what the law really was.

On the conclusion of this campaign, the
importance of West Point became more the
object of attention, and General Washington
·the better to guard this Gibraltar of America,
as it was not inaptly termed, removed his
head quarters to New Windsor, in the vicinity ; so that from the window where I
was confined, I had the daily mortification

to see the troop of horse which conveyed me
from the camp of Totowa Bridge to Stony
Point, pass and repass with some new unhappy victim to political rage, not without
apprehension that some severe measures, in
consequence of tampering with any new
witnesses, might again place me under military tyranny. One morning as I was ruminating on my miserable situation, I was
roused by my goal door being suddenly
forced open, and I was challenged by the
sheriff to know if I had any hand in the
business of aiding the Tory prisoners to
affect their escape from the dungeon?
Alarmed at the question, and the information it communicated, I replied, That
he well knew from my infirm state, it was
impossible I could give them any assistance;
this he granted, but said, in reply, that
although I could render them no personal
assistance, I might direct some of my agents
to do it? adding, that he would take care,

I should have no further communication
with any person, and that I might expect
a military guard again very soon, to take
charge of me.   In this state of mental apprehension I was detained, for some time.

The circumstance here alluded to was as
follows :—There were a number of persons
who were taken in arms, amounting to some
hundreds, who were going to join the King's
troops in Canada ; these were residents of
the Western settlements, where the country
being thinly inhabited, they had no jails,
or, at least, none large and strong enough to
contain the number of persons that were captured, and who were therefore brought to
this place for greater security.   Among them
were some of the most daring and hardy
people, belonging to Colonel Brand and
Butler's corps of Whites and Indians ; fifty
of these were crowded in a small cell, which
had a window grated with strong bars of

iron, and a centinel to watch it. Notwithstanding his vigilance, however, some implements were conveyed to the prisoners,
who, in the night, by gentle degrees, picked
away the mortar from the heavy foundation-
stones, and in the course of one night, made
an aperture large enough to admit a man of
almost any size to pass through, which they
all did, and effected their escape.

To this event I was presumed to be an
accomplice, and was consequently watched
with more severity, as well as deprived of
those occasional indulgences to which I had
been accustomed.

About this time the quarter sessions and
county court sat, when I petitioned it for
my discharge by proclamation, which was,
heretofore, the law of the land, while,
two courts having previously sat, I was
clearly entitled to the prayer of the petition.

The answer to it, however, was, that I could not be heard, nor the prayer of the petition granted, until the direction of the commissioners of conspiracy had been obtained.

I will here beg leave to remark, that the warrant of my commitment to the sheriff, was for my safe custody, until discharged by due course of law.—Here, again, was another violation of the ancient system of law, and directly repugnant to the new constitution of the state.

Soon after this was another conspiracy found out, consisting of a number of persons, who were supposed to be sent from New York, to persuade the blacks to desert from their masters, in this part of the country; great numbers of whom, availing themselves of the British troops being in possession of Stony Point, which lay contiguous to the mountains of the Highlands, had plundered their masters, sought refuge in that part, and afterwards gone to New York, where they were emancipated. A farmer, in the vicinity of the jail, having retaken one of these black renegadoes, who, through the channel described, was endeavouring to make himself as independent as his master, had confined him in it, in the hope of bringing him to a sense of his duty. He was (considering the few advantages he had had of improving his mind,) possessed of singular endowments; and had safficient address to persuade his master, that if he would permit his hand-cuffs to be taken off, he would return home with him, and faithfully re-enter into his service. The master, who felt disposed to relax in his severity, ordered the irons to be removed; but wished to have some better proof of his sincerity than his mere word, and, therefore, still kept him in confinement, fearing, as he was a desperate

fellow, he might do him, or his family, some
injury; for when re-taken, he was in company with another, who had left the famous
blockhouse, near Fort Lee, in Bergon woods,
and, in revenge for former ill usage, had
privately passed through the wood, and
shot his master.

This was the blockhouse so very unsuc-
cessfully attacked by General Wayne, with
the flower of the Continental troops, defended principally by negroes, deserters from
their masters, and which was the subject of
the severe satirical poem, called the " Cow
Chace," written by the unfortunate Major
Andre.

The black man being thus indulged by
his master, by degrees had greater liberties
granted him, preparatory to his being taken
home; he was permitted to do menial offices
for the jail-keeper, into whose confidence he

s

had insinuated himself, and thereby was entrusted with delivering the provisions to the
prisoners, and was the person who provided
those, I have mentioned, with the tools, by
which they effected their escape from the
dungeon.

Being among the number of unfortunate
prisoners confined in that jail, I found this
man, in the absence of my servant, very
useful and attentive, in rendering me many
little services, for which he would receive no
remuneration, and which, being observed
by the jailor, engendered a strong suspicion
of my being a party in the plot; but this suspicion did not end here : it was industriously
circulated that there were evidences who
were prepared to prove it; and I was cre-
dibly informed that a deserter from the convention troops had actually sworn before a
justice of the peace, that he overheard me
advise this black man to make his escape as

soon as he could, and that I had offered him
money to help him on his way to New York,
as well as to give him directions where he
might be secreted on the road, and procure
a guide through the mountains.

Alarmed at these infamous designs, I determined to lose no time in contriving
the means for my own security, by every
opportunity that should offer. A few days
after, another special court of oyer and terminer and general goal delivery was notified
to sit, and the supreme court of judicature
for the trial of causes, with an accompanying
jurisdiction within a fortnight.

I therefore, sought the earliest opportunity to inform my wife of my determination
to effect my escape: she did not long he-
sitate to come to me from Haverstraw and
confirm me in my resolution.

There was a lady in the village who had
given me assurances that if once I could
find an opportunity to quit the jail, she
would secure me until I could procure a
guide to conduct me in safety to any place
of security. This lady had long sympathized
in my distresses; she had suffered much
by the war, particularly on account of
the loss of her husband, whose life had
been most unjustly taken away for his
allegiance to his sovereign. Mrs. Smith
in consequence, informed her of my determination. Fortunately, a few days after,
several persons came to see me, as well on
business as from friendship, and they having
interest with the deputy sheriff, persuaded
him to suffer me to come out of my place of
confinement, and sit with them in the open
court room, in order to transact some business of a pecuniary nature. As the
bottle was moving briskly round, I
thought it a good opportunity to favour

my design; there were three in company; and two of them, who were rigid democrats, had become quite inebriated, while the other, my particular friend, was not much better. I affected to be in the same situation. It was now the evening of the 22^d of May and nearly dark ; Mrs. Smith, who had that day been permitted to sit with me in my place of confinement, was anxiously waiting to see if I could avail myself of a favourable opportunity ; she sent our servant to say she wished to speak to me, and would not detain me a moment. I apologised to my companions, who readily excused my absence, expecting my speedy return. When I came near the door of my prison, I suddenly turned, and, from a wink of my servant, went down a stair-case that was at the side of it, and without delay made to the outer door of the jail, which, not being bolted, I went out, and made all the haste I could, in my very weak state, to

a church-yard, not far distant, hoping to
shelter myself behind the tomb-stones, until
any search, that might take place, should be
over; I had not reached the spot more than
ten minutes, when I saw the jailor quietly
light my companions out, and wish them a
good night; they immediately mounted their
horses, and rode gently away,

I was astonished that no search was made
after me, but knowing the address of Mrs.
Smith, I presumed she had exercised her
best management; for, as soon as she was
told by the servant of the course I had taken
down the stairs, she sent him immediately
to inform my companions, that I was too
much disguised to rejoin them, and had laid
down; they, therefore, quietly came to the
door, wished her a good night, and then
mentioned the state they left me in to the
jailor, who went up, locked the jail-door,
and supposed all was right.

It now became dark,—and as the jail was fixed at the Point, where four roads met, I had to cross two of them to obtain the place of my appointment, and had nearly gained the second, when I heard the jail-door open, and shut very hard, and, soon after, the sound of persons, as if running with speed ; I knew that, by crossing a fence, I should soon gain a brook, which, at that season, was generally full of water; fear aided my steps, and having reached the stream, I boldly plunged in, gained the opposite bank, and leaning my head against it, could clearly distinguish the sound of people passing the road I had just crossed; I continued in this state until after midnight, before I thought it prudent to move, for the court being to sit so soon, they generally brought to the town a great concourse of people, to be in readiness for their different avocations, preparatory to trials, &c. At length I proceeded to the house of my protectress, who,

with a sister, were in waiting for my reception, and who received me with tears of sympathy on seeing the wet and forlorn state I
was in, without hat or shoes. They instantly warmed some strong cider with gin-
ger for me; after this refreshment they provided me with a pair of blankets, and conducted me to a shed, as a place of security,
where there was some straw, and advised
me to take rest—but the balmy friend
was a stranger to my tortured mind, from
the anxieties which agitated me for the
safety of my amiable wife, who, I knew,
from the extreme delicacy of her mind and
frame, would suffer in her state of confinement, and be solicitous for my safety.
She did, indeed, undergo much alarm; but
having a faithful servant with her, she kept
him in conversation during the night, which
greatly beguiled the time, and helped to
mitigate the horrors of the place. When
the jailor opened the door in the morning,

the servant was ready to take up her small
trunk ; my wife met him at the door, wished
him a good morning, and, passing him with
the servant, left him to look for me in the
bed, which she had formed to have the appearance of a person lying in it. Before he
had discovered that the bird was flown, she
was out of the jail ; and proceeding directly
to the clergyman of the town, threw herself
upon his protection. He assured her that,
while under his roof, he would prevent her
from receiving any injury, though he might
not be her surety against insult from the ignorant rabble, nor could he say how far he
might be implicated in law, but that he
would exert himself to the utmost in her
behalf, as a sincere friend to the family.

This clergyman was a humane and good
man ; he was an orthodox Calvinist, a warm
advocate for the independence of America,
and, being the only clergyman in the town,

he, for the two last reasons, possessed great
influence, and was therefore better able to
protect Mrs. Smith, than any other person
she could have applied to in her dilemma.

She had scarcely taken refreshment, when
she was followed by the sheriff. He had
previously been to the inn, where, finding
her carriage and horses, he seized them for
confiscation; and her servant, the same
that was in jail with her, informed him
where his mistress was to be found, when
all being secured, he came in quest of her.
His first address, on entering the clergyman's house, was insolent in the highest degree; he was, however, checked by her venerable friend, and becoming more moderate, he declared that if she did not instantly
inform him where her husband was, he
would detain her until I was secured; that
he would have me, dead or alive; that he
had parties out on every road; and that those

who succeeded in my apprehension, would receive one hundred dollars for their trouble. Finding herself protected, Mrs. Smith boldly answered, that she had reason to believe I was by that time far out of his reach, that in what she had done she was well advised by the first counsel at law in the state, and defied the exercise of his power as a sheriff, in any thing he could or might do to her prejudice. In much passion he then left her, charging the clergyman not to suffer her departure until he returned, saying, that the attorney-general was shortly to be in the town of Goshen, and that he should take his _ advice on the subject.

The worthy clergyman, with the tenderest humanity, endeavoured to console Mrs. Smith in this embarrassed situation, and succeeded in persuading her to take some rest, which she had not long enjoyed, when she was disturbed by the sheriff, accom-

panied by the state's attorney; they exerted
their combined rhetoric to persuade her to
reveal the place of refuge I had sought, and
what route I had taken; finding this of no
effect to gain any information, they added
threats, and declared, they would confine
her in case of non-compliance; but all this
proving ineffectual, they left her in the custody of the clergyman, in the full expectation of my apprehension.

Knowing that I was in good hands, and
that no further aid could be rendered on her
part, Mrs. Smith availing herself of the absence of the sheriff, and to rid herself of any
further importunity, hired a coach, and proceeded to her family at Haverstraw.

The whole of this procedure was detailed
to me the ensuing evening, to my no small
satisfaction, that matters had so far terminated well; though my joy was not un-

mixed with pain at the reflection, that so
amiable a woman had to encounter so much
misery.

The shock of my first arrest, and near nine
months imprisonment, together with the
loss of almost all our property, affected Mrs.
Smith to such a degree, as brought on a decline, which she never recovered ; and she
might truly be said to have died a martyr to
grief.

During my residence in this jail, I had
many offers to procure my enlargement, but
there was no one to be trusted.   One unfortunate prisoner, who endeavoured to
escape, was betrayed by his guide, and
carried before General Washington.   Another, through the ignorance of his guide,
mistaking his route, was taken upon the
lines, and, as well as his conductor, was

brought back, tried, and sentenced to imprisonment during the war.

After Mrs. Smith's departure, the most
diligent search was made to discover me.
Parties were sent in different directions from
the four roads that led from the jail; but on
their return without success, it was concluded, I must be secreted in the town,
among the King's friends, who were by far
the most numerous and respectable of the
inhabitants.   On the evening of the third
day, before my good protectress had any hint
of the measure, a young lady came hastily
to her, and informed her, that a few hours
ago her father's house had been searched,
and she had heard the party say, they should
next take the road where my good friend
lived; she instantly came to me with the
intelligence, and advised my leaving the
place where I was for another more secure,

which was a hollow between two stacks of chimnies; this I did not approve of, as the place had a suspicious appearance, and seemed to me calculated for a hiding-place I therefore observed, that as it was near the evening, I would go out to the woods, and return when dark ; I had scarcely mentioned my resolution, when the young lady called to her, and said the guards were very near the house,—when instantly snatching up one of my blankets, I stept lightly down the stairs, she following with the other blan-ket; we heard the tramp of a number of steps in the piazza ;—I made immediately to the back-door, and crept under a small hen-coop; she hastily threw her blanket over it, —and, turning round, met the party coming in at the front-door. My protectress being a suspected person, from the reasons I have already mentioned, her house was searched with great care; and the young lady after wards informed me, that in the very hole where she wished me to secret myself, they thrust their bayonets and pikes; so that had I been there, I must, inevitably, have been put to death! The house being thoroughly searched, they proceeded to the barn, stables, and even the pig-sty; and passing the hen-coop, under which I was concealed, they were about to take off the blanket, when my protectress exclaimed, " For God's sake do not hurt my poor chickens;" on which they went into the house, and I could hear them distinctly charge her with knowing where I was; alarmed, lest her fears might overcome her fortitude, I immediately crept out, and made the best of my way to an adjoining wood, under the cover of darkness, which had commenced.

Having reached the wood, I was involved in doubt what course to take; to go back did not seem prudent, as on my return, some soldiers might be left as a guard; it now began to rain, and fortunately a large hollow tree offered me a shelter from its rage. A variety of conflicting passions agitated my mind; for that very night a person was to come and bring me clothing, and take me part of my way to New York, upwards of eighty miles. To omit profiting by this chance, I knew, would be imprudent; and the person I expected had promised to assist me, and possessed my most unlimited confidence. At length it occurred to me that the lady, from whose house I had just escaped, had a relation about five miles distant: I knew him to be a kind, friendly man, to whom I could commit myself with safety. Thither, therefore, I determined to proceed; and when in the main road, I thought I could easily reach his house. I travelled all night; it rained during the whole time; and my feet being tender, from the distressing and unusual state in which I was placed, I made but little

T

progress, especially along a slaty and rocky
country. When I had walked a considerable distance I halted, intending to wait for
the dawn of day ; this advancing slowly, I
seated myself on a rock, faint, fatigued,
and lacerated with briars, and passed my
time in lamenting the hard fate which my
civility to a stranger had intailed upon
me.

On the approach of day I saw something
like a house, and the appearance of light ;
I advanced towards it ;—the reader will here
again form some faint idea of my sensations,
when I found the spot was near the gibbet,
and the house I had discerned was the jail,
from whence I had escaped in the dark. I
had lost my road ; and in my bewildered
state of mind, had the whole night been
wandering back again, over the same
ground!! Afflicted, dismayed, and almost
exhausted, I had no other alternative than

to return to the place from whence I had last
escaped—and now gave up all for lost! It
was, however, fortunate that I had not far
to go, for day-light rapidly advanced ; and I
omitted no time in regaining the good woman's house, having the main road before
me; and being equally fortunate in not
meeting a single traveller, or my forlorn
appearance must have attracted notice, and,
perhaps, have led to a discovery.

I observed, on my approach, that there
was light in the house, and once more assuming courage, fortified by hope, I ventured
to tap gently at a window from whence the
light appeared, and, in a minute, the door
was opened for my reception. My female
friend informed me, that the party, who
had been there the preceding day, were not
satisfied with their first search, but insisted
on making another by candle-light, which
they did, and even commanded her to open

every closet, chest, and trunk, declaring
they had authority to confine her, unless
she told them where I was,—and that one of
them even went again to the chicken-coop,
under which I had been concealed, and
thrust his bayonet into various parts of it.
She said it was well I overheard the conversation, and resolved to withdraw ; and she
consoled me by saying, I now had nothing
to fear, as they had gone away perfectly
satisfied,   I mentioned my attempt to reach
the residence of her relation for shelter, and
I had the pleasure to learn that there I should
have been safe; but it was providential that
I missed my way, for a large party of Continental troops were encamped not far from
his house, and I must have passed them
before I could arrive at it.

Combining all these circumstances, which
appeared so providential, I was led, independent of the fatigue I had just passed

through, to take some rest in my former birth, with renewed ground to encourage hope.

My friend had promised to be with me the following night, but when that came I was sorely disappointed. Through a chink in the place of my retreat, I could see the members of the court, judge, jury, and all, pass and repass; and, indeed, I was every moment in dread of being discovered, and brought back to my old quarters. In this situation I continued, however, five days, under the most painful apprehensions.

At length my guide arrived; he had been very prudently employed in reconnoitring the road, before he would venture to conduct me. He appointed the ensuing evening for my escape, and came punctually, well armed and mounted, with a change of dress for myself, a complete disguise. I had no sooner equipped myself, than throw-ing a woman's cloak over me, he took me up behind him, on a strong horse:—we went ten miles that night, without any in-terruption, meeting many persons we both knew, with whom he conversed; but they, supposing me to be a woman, some relation of my friend's, did not direct their discourse to me; he was prepared, if they had done so, to tell them that the woman was deaf! The name of the place, where we halted, was Chester, and the man of the house was nicknamed the *whisperer*, from the circum-stance of his speaking so loud in common conversation, as to be heard at a very great distance. If he had addressed me, I should have been reduced to an aukward dilemma; as my pretended deafness would have been no subterfuge. However, he took no notice of me, a neglect for which I felt much obligation.

From the whisperer's we proceeded through a part of the Highland Mountains, passing Sterling and Ringwood iron-works, to the confines of Pumpton Plains, to the house of a man who was one of the king's warmest friends, and among the Dutch inhabitants, famed for being double-jointed, as well as an ambidexter. We found the house crowded with Continental troops; my friend observing the crowd, went in, leaving me at a small distance; the landlord soon came out, and directed us to a small hovel, at the end of his farm, where he promised he would come, and bring us refreshment; he was not gone long, when he returned, and informed us we must change our route, for that the road we proposed going, across Pumpton Plains, was filled with troops going to and from camp, and advised my friend to go towards Paulshook, especially as he did not understand the Dutch language, the dialect spoken in that part. This we thought most advisable; and my friend took his departure, leaving me in the ambidexter's confidence and pro-, tection.

The succeeding night, the ambidexter came to me with a good horse, and another for himself; we had then to pass a narrow defile, between two mountains; and he mentioned to me, that possibly we might at that place be challenged by a centinel, to whom he would answer, and that I might ride on briskly, there being no turning on the road, and he would soon overtake me. When we had gone about five miles, we were suddenly challenged—" Who comes there?" He answered, " Friends;" and rode up to the person. I gave my horse a free rein, and pressed on; soon after I heard the discharge of a musket, and was overtaken by ambidexter, who, passing, called to me to come on as fast as possible; he had not rode a mile, when, following close, I saw him turn up on the left, through the woods, in a narrow path, whither I followed. We soon dismounted; and, after tying the horses to a tree in the valley, he led me through the roughest road imaginable, path intersecting path, and, from an eminence, shewed me, when day appeared, Tatowa Bridge: he then left me, to go and seek a friend, who would be mine also. It was near night before he returned, accompanied by two men, who were to see me safe into Ponter's Hook. They brought some provision, and a bottle of spirits, and observed, that they went weekly to New York with country produce, and requested to know what I would give them for their trouble? I shewed them six moidores, which, I said, was all I then had, but would make up any sum they thought right, when we came to New York. Having previously paid ambidexter, I took my leave of him. He told my guides in

low Dutch, which I understood, that he
was stopped on the road by the centinel,
who attempted to seize the bridle of his
horse, saying, " that is Smith that has
passed," upon which ambidexter jerked the
horse's head aside, and gave the centinel a
severe blow on the arm, and then left him,
to join me. Ambidexter (whom I have
seen since, as well as the two men, my new
pilots,) recommended me to their special
care, assuring them he knew me, and saying, they would be well paid, if they conveyed me safe. We lost no time in going
down a steep hill, which brought us by a
short cut to Totowa Bridge.

My reflections and sensations in passing
this bridge, which I had so often crossed to
and from my trial, were painful, from the
various ideas that successively passed in my
mind. One of the men, turning to the
other, said in Dutch, " he may now think

himself safe, for the damned rebels don't often pass that bridge, except in numbers; for fear of accident, we will take the mountain-road." Here they stopped; and then turning to me, one of them said, " Friend, we must now give you some directions. As we should be suspected if three of us were seen together, I will go first, nearly out of sight; you follow next, but be sure you have me in view; if you hear me sing loud, you must jump out of the road into the bushes; then my partner, having his eye upon you, and seeing you do that, immediately runs to me, knowing that some person is coming forward; if they have seen but two persons on the road, and my partner supplies your place, the two persons are there still:—On the other hand, if he hears or sees any person coming after him, he sings, and you must do the same, go into the bushes, and he will run to supply your place; I stand still; and, on their coming,

the two persons seen are my partner and
myself."

Understanding them perfectly well,
(though, perhaps, these cautionary arrangements may not be sufficiently clear to the
reader,) we went on, and, in a few hours,
reached Aquakinac, on the banks of the
Passaic, or, as some call it, Second River,
over which is built Totowa Bridge.

Here we entered the house of one of my
pilots; and only in two instances was I
obliged to go out of the road, and this was
caused by persons whom we met, but from
none that overtook us. I was put into a
private room, where I had every thing that
I could wish for.

At length the happy period arrived, when
I was to take the last stage of my journey;
and on the evening of the 4th of June, 1782,

my two pilots crossed this river in a small cedar canoe, or boat, to the opposite shore, which was a salt meadow, sometimes overflowed by the tide, which leaves a muddy slime, over which a light boat may easily be drawn. We passed a large tract of meadow, some miles in length, before we came to another river, called Hackinsack River, on the opposite shore of which, near the foot of Snake Hill, we discovered a party of men, who hailed us;—not answering, they fired several shot, but they fell far short of us. We now judged it prudent to hide the boat in the sedges, and retire, as they could not pass to us; this being done, we hid ourselves,—and, soon after, heard several vollies, appearing to us as if two parties had been attacking each other; this ceasing, we again ventured to the margin of the river, and observing no person on or near the opposite shore, we boldly launched our bark, knowing that no parties but British would

venture to stay there long in broad day-
light; we crossed in safety, and soon reached
the town of Bergen, where halting a few
minutes for refreshment, we proceeded to
Pryor's Mills, near Paulshook, and were
informed by the man of the house, that
owing to fresh orders that had been given
by Sir Henry Clinton, no person would be
permitted to enter New York by that post.
Situated as I was, I determined to apply to
the centinel; he detained me and the pilots
until his relief came, when I wrote a note
to the commanding officer, who was fortunately colonel of the same regiment that
Major Andre belonged to. While detained
here, Captain Moody came in with a captured mail of General Washington's dispatches; and, soon after, a serjeant and file
arrived to carry us across the ferry. From
my disguise, he would not believe me to be
the person I avowed myself to be; but as
the mail was immediately to go to New

York, he promised to report me to the commander in chief: his secretary, however,
gave me directions where to find my brother, the chief-justice, he being intimate with
the family; and, in a short time after, I was
permitted to cross with Captain Moody,
and was paraded before head-quarters.   My
brother was a near neighbour to Sir Henry
Clinton, and his servant, seeing me, told
my brother of my situation, who applied to
Sir Henry in my behalf, and took me, to
my no small joy, to his house.

In a few weeks after my arrival, to add to
my wretchedness, my family, deprived of
their all, were banished to New York.   I
continued with my brother for several
months, endeavouring to obtain some of my
own houses, and others belonging to the
family estate, which Lieutenant-General
Robertson, then being governor, put into
my possession.   I continued in the exercise

of my profession, until the evacuation of
New York by the British troops, when,
through the assistance of Sir Guy Carlton,
now Lord Dorchester, I was enabled to obtain my passage to England in the Ann,
transport, of Whitby, in Yorkshire, under
convoy of the Guiana, frigate, (as appears
from his lordship's order to Thomas Aston
Coffin, Esq. the present commissary-gene-
ral, then paymaster of contingencies at
New York, from the Audit-Office, Somerset
Place,) and landed at Falmouth, in twenty-
one days, from New York, which I left on
the 5th of November, 1783. This ship returned a part of the first division of auxiliary troops, commanded by Colonel Be-
zenrodt, who charged me with dispatches to
the Right Honourable Lord North; and, on
my arrival in London, I placed them in the
hands of my friend and agent, Gray Elliott,
Esq. then Keeper of Plantation Records, at
Whitehall, who kindly procured accom-

modations for me in Surry-Street, in the
Strand.

I had not long arrived, before I received
an afflicting account of the death of my wife,
who, from the first shock, upon my being
arrested by order of Washington, had been
daily declining in health, which increased
in consequence of my compulsive departure
at the end of the war, and which terminated
her existence on the 1st of January, 1784,
with a truly broken heart; leaving me, her
disconsolate survivor, with two helpless children, after an intercourse of ten years' un-
interrupted harmony—an exile, devoid of
the soothing consolations of friendship.
This last afflictive dispensation, added to the
series of calamities I had heretofore endured,
prostrated all the barriers philosophy had
raised; melancholy had enveloped my mind,
and I was sinking in the glooms of despair,
viewing every object through the most ap-

U

palling medium; when, providentially, Sir
Egerton Leigh, with whom I had the honour
of an acquaintance in America, found my
residence; by his polite and friendly as-
siduities, I was roused from a stupor, that
had, for the time, destroyed all rational reflections. I was slowly recovering from this
baneful reverie, when I was unexpectedly
visited by General Arnold. The sudden in-
trusion of the man who had occasioned my
miseries, excited sensations that I cannot
describe, and which I leave to the sugges-
tions of a candid world. The reception
which he experienced from me, (as publicly
mentioned by Captain Roorback, of General
Delancey's regiment of New York Loyalists,) shortened the interview.

As I have often mentioned this general,
whose conduct and character, whilst the
memory of the American war exists, will be
the subject of animadversion; I will here re-

late some, circumstances in contradiction to
the opinion generally entertained respecting
him ; not that I mean to advocate measures,
which are alone justifiable from the secret
motives which influenced their operations ;
but I wish that the candid reader may be
enabled to form his own opinion from the
contrast of the characters drawn.

In one of my first interviews with General Arnold, he ludicrously mentioned that
he had been stiled by some of the American
army a jockey and horse-dealer ; this he
denied to have been his original profession ;
but declared, he was brought up to the
business of an apothecary, which Old Thun-
der-Rod, as the Americans call Doctor
Franklin, (who derived such merit from ex-
periments in electricity, collected from the
hints of the immortal Sir Isaac Newton,)
avers to be the fact ; and that he was educated for the profession by Dr. Lothrop, of

Connecticut, a gentleman of eminence, and
estimable character; who, for the fidelity
the general displayed during his apprentice-
ship, retained him in his employ a considerable time afterwards, as a mark of his esteem;
and, in remuneration for his diligent services, gave him a reward of £.500 sterling.
Being of an active disposition, and detesting
the languor of still life, he relinquished the
business of an apothecary; and, having acquired a competent knowledge of navigation,
he embarked his property in the trade
usually carried on between the continent and
the West Indian islands, reciprocally beneficial to each, with various loss and gain,
until the disturbances between Great Britain in 1774, when he stepped forward the
champion of his country's cause; and for
the zeal he discovered for its prosperity,
was appointed a colonel by the legisiature
of that government. Political disputes in-
creasing, daily afforded, on the appeal to

arms as the arbiter, full exercise for the natural activity of his disposition; and early in
the succeeding year, he commanded a detachment of militia, to prevent the irrup-
tions of the Canadians and Savages on Lake
Champlain.   His indefatigable exertions
secured his success; in consideration of
which Congress confirmed the appointment
he received from the provincial authority.
The intrepidity of his genius induced that
body to invest him with the separate command of a corps of troops, amounting to
twelve hundred choice men, with whom he
was directed, on the 13th of November,
1775, to cross the Wilderness, from the
camp at Cambridge, for the invasion of
Canada; and, notwithstanding the most
fatiguing hardships, as I have already mentioned, he arrived before the walls of Quebec
on the 13th of November, regardless of the
approaching inclement season, and summoned the town to surrender, with which

it would certainly have complied, from the
lukewarmness of the Canadians in general,
had not this requisition been incompatible
with the duty and invincible firmness of
the brave and experienced officer who commanded the garrison; and on the junction of
General Montgomery, on the 15th of December following, the siege was commenced with
spirit, and subsequently Quebec was stormed;
the issue of which, from the gallant and judicious defence made by the besieged, is well
known;—Montgomery was killed—Arnold
wounded, and most of the besiegers made
prisoners of war; the clemency they received from Lord Dorchester—the lenient
treatment, and the affecting advice, (instead
of warlike rigour) he administered to the
prisoners, on dismissing them peaceably to
their respective homes, had the most con-
ciliating effect, at once coinciding with the
humanity, as well as bravery, of their distinguished conqueror.

On the march of General Montgomery to
join General Arnold, or by the detachment
under Colonel Ethan Allen, the unfortunate
Major Andre was captured, and sent as a
prisoner, with his brother-officers, through
a large extent of the American continent,
to Trenton, in New Jersey. I remember
having seen him at the hospitable table of
Colonel Hay, at Haverstraw, whose urbanity was dispensed to all genteel travellers,
but I did not recollect the least trace of his
countenance when I received him from the
Vulture sloop of war. This event enabled
him to form some idea of the genius, temper,
and political disposition of the American
people; and it was in this situation that he
made the reference to his amiable friend's
picture, which he stiled his talisman.

But I must return from this digression to
the character of General Arnold.—He assured me he was descended from a gentle-

man of the same name, who was one of the
first Governors of Rhode Island, but his
immediate progenitor, by occasion of many
losses in trade, failed, some time before his
death, leaving the general to the wide world
friendless and unprotected. Determined to
be the *faber suæ fortunæ*, he lost no opportunity that offered ; and when they did not
take notice of him, he courted them by all
honest exertions to advance his fortunes,
holding in view the poet's sentiment :

> Honour and fame from no condition rise,
> Act well your part—there all the honour lies.

The ingratitude and injustice of his countrymen, and the illiberal treatment his lady
received from Mr. Read, the Governor of
Pennsylvania, were among the reasons he
assigned, in his declaration, for his defection, and which he deemed sufficient to
alienate his attachment from a cause wherein
the private interest of a few leading individuals seemed to him to be more the ob-

ject contemplated, in protracting the war, (after the overtures of the peace-commissioners of 1778 had done away all obstacles to a permanent re-union of the empire, upon the broad basis of reciprocal benefits,) than the good of his fellow-citizens, whom he saw plunged into the most forlorn misery, from which nothing but the relenting clemency and generosity of the British government could extricate them—and not the perfidious allurements of their impotent ally, who looked with a covetous eye to the re-possession of their former territory in Canada, from which they were averted by the vigilance of Washington, who penetrated their designs, and wisely avoided miseries similar to those he experienced in Braddock's defeat.

Mankind differ as much in their political as religious sentiments. It is a proof of an ingenuous mind to retract from error, the

moment it is discovered. These sentiments
General Arnold avowed as the cause of his
change of views, and not the *auri sacra
fames*, with which, it is said, Doctor Franklin charged him;—but he, likewise, has
met with his political enemies, who assert
that, with his coadjutor, Tom Paine, he
disseminated those principles which deluged
his country in blood. The philosopher, as
well as the soldier, has paid the debt to
Nature—peace to their manes! Political
prejudices are, of all others, the most diffi-
cult to be removed. There never was a
contest that admitted more pretext for diver-
sity of opinion:—General Arnold's conduct
is reprobated by some, and as strongly ad-
vocated by others; not standing upon the
same eminence of information, all men do
not see with equal light;—both friends and
enemies, however, concur in doing justice
to General Arnold's merit, as a man of rare
valour, and a gallant officer.

To delineate the character of the unfortunate Major Andre—to view him in the vivacity of his fancy, the elegance of his taste, or the powers of his mind, in all the rich felicities of his genius, as a literary character, or his military capacity, in both maturing to the highest eclat, and to render tributary justice to his worth, requires talents beyond common eulogy. The virtuous and liberal contemplate, with intellectual luxury, the meritorious dispositions of their fellow-citizens; the principles of benevolence they possessed, expand and elevate our ideas of the human character,— and, while we analise their superior excellence, stimulate to copy their bright example, and direct our views to the Author of all that is estimable in man.

The portrait of Major Andre presents the image of his mind, and is the index of the goodness of his heart. To those who knew

him, the animation of his countenance, the
impressive force of his genius, the graceful-
ness of his manner, the enlivening intelligence of his converse, is at once expressed
and felt—he was rapid in his penetration,
and expansive in his comprehension—his
intellectual resources, from the clearness
of his conception and arrangement, were
promptly at command; hence, with a natural desire to please, the attractions of his
personal accomplishments gave a zest and
charm to his conversation, and soon con-
verted simple esteem into the dignity of
friendship—urbanity, in its highest extent,
was a qualification of the least intrinsic
value he possessed—the scrupulous rectitude of his mind, the truth and inviolable
integrity of his heart, invariably governed
by reason, and sanctioned by religion, regu-
lated his principles of honour, and were
conspicuous in the habits of his life—his
social conviviality was uncontaminated by

intemperance, and levity or indecorum at
no time sullied his wit or gaiety—his extensive knowledge of human nature, and command of himself, qualified him as the
soothing companion of the afflicted, to be
serious with the elderly, sprightly with the
gay, and facetious with the juvenile—by his
learning he softened the austerities of philosophy; and his taste in selecting his
amusements, gave an additional pleasure to
their enjoyment—his beneficence was en-
hanced by the prompt anticipation of the
favour he meant to confer; and his denials
were mitigated by a suavity of manner, that
almost seemed a compliance of favour—to
him might justly be applied the reputation
given of Agricola by Tacitus,—" *Quicquid
ex Agricola amavimus, quicquid mirati su-
mus, manet mansurumque est in animis
hominum.*

Whatever in Andre was the object of our

love and admiration, remains; and will remain in the hearts of all who knew him.
With such qualifications, added to the bril-
liancy of his military talents, which invited
the esteem and patronage of Sir Henry Clinton, (whose happiness was ever to reward
merit,) who could be surprised that his virtues, and the gallant spirit with which he
terminated his career, should deserve the
monument erected to his memory—impe-
riously extract the involuntary tear—and
demand the panegyric of an enemy?—Or
even inspire the elegant pencil of England's
favourite Muse, to celebrate the deathless
name of a British officer, whose prowess
and talents will live in the memory of the
brave, the generous, and the good, as long
as the historic page shall record his unsullied fame?

Britons know how to judge, appreciate,
and grant the laureled meed, to decorate the

brow of genuine worth ; nor will there ever
be wanting among the gallant race those
who will cherish the memory, imitate the
virtues, and sprinkle with the tributary tear
the ashes of departed merit.—" *Non cane-*
mus surdis respondent et omniæ silviæ.

I shall finally conclude this narrative
with the following documents, which will
satisfy many individuals to whom I am unknown, as to the sense which the Government at that time entertained of my unme-
rited sufferings on their account, and which
will also completely refute the gross calumny
which, at the commencement of this volume,
I quoted from a public magazine :—

Certificates by Order of the Honourable
Board of Commissioners for Auditing
Public Accounts.

I hereby certify, that upon the examina

tion of the vouchers belonging to the declared account of Colonel Roger Morris, Inspector of Claims of Refugees at New York, it appears that Joshua H. Smith, Esq. was allowed a Dollar *per diem*, pursuant to the orders of their Excellencies Sir Henry Clinton, K. B. and Sir Guy Carlton, K. B. commanders in chief in North America, in the years 1781, and 1782.

Audit-Office, Somerset-   J. L. MALLET, *Sec.*
Place, Oct. 26. 1807.

And it also appears in the declared account of Thomas Aston Coffin, Esq. as Paymaster of Contingencies at New York and Halifax, from the 1st of February, 1783, to the 24th of April, 1784, that Joshua H. Smith, Esq. was allowed at the rate of Seven Shillings *per diem*, from the 1st of January, to the 31st of March, 1783; and from

thence to the 31st of December following; which last payment was to enable
him to return to England, by order of
the Commander in Chief, Sir Guy
Carlton, K. B.

Audit-Office, Somerset-   I. L. MALLET, *Sec.*
Place, Jan. 19, 1808.

CONCLUSION OF THE NARRATIVE.

A

MONODY

ON THE DEATH OF

MAJOR JOHN ANDRE,

BY MISS SEWARD.

HIS EXCELLENCY

SIR HENRY CLINTON,

KNIGHT OF THE BATH.

SIR

WITH the zeal of a religious enthusiast to his murdered saint, the author of this mournful eulogium consecrates it to the memory of Major Andre, who fell a martyr in the cause of his king and country, with the firm intrepidity of a Roman, and the amiable resignation of a Christian hero.

Distant awe and reverence prevent her offering these effusions of gratitude to the beneficent and royal patron of the Andre family. May Mr. Andre's illustrious general, the guardian of his injured honour, his conspicuous and personal friend, deign to accept them from One, who was once happy in the friendship of the GLORIOUS SUFFERER.

Your Excellency's

most obedient humble servant,

ANNA SEWARD.

TO MISS SEWARD.

IMPROMPTU.

AS Britain mourn'd, with all a mother's pain,
Two sons, two gallant sons, ignobly slain!
Mild Cook, by savage fury robb'd of breath,
And martial Andre doom'd to baser death!
The Goddess, plung'd in grief too vast to speak,
Hid in her robe her tear-disfigur'd cheek.

The sacred Nine, with sympathetic care,
Survey'd the noble mourner's dumb despair;
While from their choir the sighs of pity broke,
The Muse of Elegy thus warmly spoke:
" Take injur'd parent, all we can bestow,
" To sooth thy heart, and mitigate thy woe!"

Speaking, to earth the kind enthusiast came,
And veil'd her heavenly power with Seward's name:
And that no vulgar eye might pierce the truth,
Proclaim'd herself the friend of Andre's youth.

In that fair semblance, with such plaintive fire,
She struck the chords of her pathetic lyre.:
The weeping Goddess owns the blest relief,
And fondly listens, with subsiding grief;
Her loveliest daughters lend a willing ear,
Honouring the latent Muse with many a tear.
Her bravest sons, who in their every vein
Feel the strong pathos of the magic strain,
Bless the inchanting lyre, by glory strung,
Envying the dead, who are so sweetly sung.

W. HAYLEY.

MONODY

ON

MAJOR ANDRE.

LOUD howls the storm! the vex'd Atlantic roars!
Thy Genius, Britain, wanders on its shores!
Hears cries of horror wafted from afar,
And groans of Anguish, mid the shrieks of War!
Hears the deep curses of the Great and Brave,
Sigh in the wind, and murmur on the wave!
O'er his damp brow the sable crape he binds,
And throws his * victor-garland to the winds;
Bids haggard Winter, in her drear sojourn,
Tear the dim foliage from her drizzling urn;
With sickly yew unfragrant cypress twine,
And hang the dusky wreath round Honour's shrine.
Bids steel-clad Valour chace his dove-like Bride,
Enfeebling Mercy, from his awful side;

---

* *Victor-garland*—Alluding to the conquest by **Lord Cornwallis.**

Where long she sat, and check'd the ardent rein,
As whirl'd his chariot o'er th' embattled plain;
Gilded with sunny smile her April tear,
Rais'd her white arm and stay'd th' uplifted spear;
Then, in her place, bids Vengeance mount the car,
And glut with gore th' insatiate Dogs of War!—
With one pale hand the * bloody scroll he rears,
And bids his Nations blot it with their tears;
And one, extended o'er th' Atlantic wave,
Points to his ANDRE's ignominious grave!

And shall the Muse, that marks the solemn scene,
" As busy Fancy lifts the veil between,"
Refuse to mingle in the awful train,
Nor breathe with glowing zeal the votive strain?
From public fame shall admiration fire
The boldest numbers of her raptur'd lyre
To hymn a Stranger?—and with ardent lay
Lead the wild Mourner round her COOK's morai,
While ANDRE fades upon his dreary bier,
And † JULIA's only tribute is her tear?

* *Bloody scroll.*—The Court-Martial decree, signed at Tappan, for Major Andre's execution.

† *Julia.*—The name by which Mr. Andre address'd the Author in his correspondence with her.

Dear, lovely Youth ! whose gentle virtues stole
Thro' Friendship's soft'ning medium on her soul !
Ah no !—with every strong resistless plea,
Rise the recorded days she pass'd with thee,
While each dim shadow of o'erwhelming years,
With Eagle-glance reverted, Memory clears.

Belov'd Companion of the fairest hours
That rose for her in Joy's resplendent bow'rs,
How gaily shone on thy bright Morn of Youth
The Star of Pleasure, and the Sun of Truth !
Full from their source descended on thy mind
Each gen'rous virtue, and each taste refin'd.
Young Genius led thee to his varied fane.
Bade thee ask * all his gifts, nor ask in vain;
Hence novel thoughts, in ev'ry lustre drest
Of pointed wit, that diamond of the breast ;
Hence glow'd thy fancy with poetic ray,
Hence music warbled in thy sprightly lay ;

* *All his gifts.*—Mr. Andre had conspicuous talents for Poetry, Music, and Painting. The Newspapers mentioned a satiric poem of his upon the Americans, which was supposed to have stimulated their barbarity towards him.——Of his wit and vivacity, the letters subjoined to this work afford ample proof. They were addressed to the author by Mr. Andre when he was a youth of eighteen.

And hence thy pencil, with his colours warm,
Caught ev'ry grace, and copied ev'ry charm,
Whose transient glories beam on Beauty's cheek,
And bid the glowing Ivory breathe and speak.
Blest pencil! by kind Fate ordain'd to save
HONORA's semblance from * her early grave,
Oh! while on † JULIA's arm it sweetly smiles,
And each lorn thought, each long regret beguiles,
Fondly she weeps the hand, which form'd the spell,
Now shroudless mould'ring in its earthy cell!

But sure the Youth, whose ill-starr'd passion strove
With all the pangs of inauspicious Love,
Full oft' deplor'd the fatal Art, that stole
The jocund freedom of its Master's soul!

While with nice hand he mark'd the living grace,
And matchless sweetness of HONORA's Face,

* *Early grave,*—Miss Honora S——, to whom Mr. Andre's
attachment was of such singular constancy, died in a consumption a few months before he suffered death at Tappan. She had married another Gentleman four years after her engagement with Mr. Andre had been dissolved by parental authority.

† *Julia's arm.*—Mr. Andre drew two miniature pictures of Miss Honora S—— on his first acquaintance with her at Buxton, in the year 1769, one for himself, the other for the author of this poem.

Th' enamour'd Youth the faithful traces blest,
That barb'd the dart of Beauty in his breast;
Around his neck th' enchanting Portrait hung,
While a warm vow burst ardent from his tongue,
That from his bosom no succeeding day,
No chance should bear that Talisman away.

'Twas thus * Apelles bask'd in Beauty's blaze,
And felt the mischief of the stedfast gaze;
Trac'd with disorder'd hand Campaspe's charms,
And as their beams the kindling Canvas warms,
Triumphant Love, with still superior art,
Engraves their wonders on the Painter's heart.

Dear lost Companion! ever constant Youth!
That Fate had smil'd propitious on thy Truth!
Nor bound th' ensanguin'd laurel on that brow
Where Love ordain'd his brightest wreath to glow!
Then Peace had led thee to her softest bow'rs,
And Hymen strew'd thy path with all his flow'rs;
Drawn to thy roof, by Friendship's silver cord,
Each social Joy had brighten'd at thy board;

* *'Twas thus Apelles.*—Prior is very elegant upon this circumstance in an Ode to his friend Mr. Howard, the painter.

Science, and soft Affection's blended rays
Had shone unclouded on thy lengthen'd days;
From hour to hour thy taste, with conscious pride,
Had mark'd new talents in thy lovely Bride;
Till thou hadst own'd the magic of her face
Thy fair HONORA's least engaging grace.
Dear lost HONORA! o'er thy early bier
Sorrowing the Muse still sheds her sacred tear!
The blushing Rose-bud in its vernal bed,
By Zephyrs fann'd, by glist'ring Dew-drops fed,
In June's gay morn that scents the ambient air,
Was not more sweet, more innocent, or fair.
Oh! when such pairs their kindred Spirit find,
When Sense and Virtue deck each spotless Mind,
Hard is the doom that shall the union break,
And Fate's dark billow rises o'er the wreck.

Now Prudence, in her cold and thrifty care,
Frown'd on the Maid, and bade the Youth despair;
For Pow'r Parental sternly saw, and strove
To tear the lily-bands of plighted Love;
Nor strove in vain;—but while the Fair-One's sighs
Disperse, like April-storms in sunny skies,
The firmer Lover, with unswerving truth,
To his first passion consecrates his Youth;

Tho' four long years a night of absence prove,
Yet Hope's soft Star shone trembling on his Love;
Till * hov'ring Rumour chas'd the pleasing dream
And veil'd with Raven-wing the silver beam.

" Honora lost! my happy rival's Bride!
" Swell ye full Sails! and roll thou mighty Tide!
" O'er the dark Waves forsaken Andre bear
" Amid the volleying Thunders of the War!
" To win bright Glory from my Country's Foes,
" E'en in this ice of Love, my bosom glows.
" Voluptuous London! in whose gorgeous bow'rs
" The frolic Pleasures lead the dancing Hours,
" From Orient-vales Sabean-odours bring,
" Nor ask her roses of the tardy Spring;
" Where Painting burns the Grecian Meed to claim,
" From the high Temple of immortal Fame,
" Bears to the radiant Goal, with ardent pace,
" Her Kauffman's Beauty, and her Reynold's grace;
" Where Music floats the glitt'ring roofs among,
" And with meand'ring cadence swells the song,
" While Sun-clad Poesy the Bard inspires,
" And foils the Grecian Harps, the Latian Lyres.—

* *Hov'ring Rumour.*—The tidings of Honora's Marriage. Upon
that event Mr. Andre quitted his profession as a merchant, and
joined our army in America.

" Ye soft'ning Luxuries! ye polish'd Arts!

" Bend your enfeebling rays on tranquil hearts!

" I quit the Song, the Pencil, and the Lyre,

" White robes of Peace, and Pleasure's soft attire,

" To seize the sword, to mount the rapid car,

,' In all the proud habiliments of War.—

" HONORA lost! I woo a sterner Bride,

" The arm'd Bellona calls me to her side;

" Harsh is the music of our marriage strain!

" It breathes in thunder from the western plain!

" Wide o'er the wat'ry world its echoes roll,

" And rouse each latent ardor of my soul.

" And tho' unlike the soft melodious lay,

" That gaily wak'd HONORA's nuptial day,

" Its deeper tones shall whisper, e'er they cease,

" More genuine transport, and more lasting peace!

" Resolv'd I go!—nor from that fatal bourn

" To these gay scenes shall ANDRE's step return!

" Set is the star of Love, that ought to guide

" His refluent Bark across the mighty Tide!

" But while my Country's Foes, with impious hand,

" Hurl o'er the blasted plains the livid brand

" Of dire Sedition! Oh! let Heav'n ordain

" While ANDRE lives, he may not live in vain!

" Yet without one kind farewel, cou'd I roam
" Far from my weeping Friends, my peaceful home,
" The best affections of my heart must cease,
" And gratitude be lost, with hope, and peace!

" My lovely Sisters! who were wont to twine
" Your souls' soft feeling with each wish of mine,
" Shall, when this breast beats high at Glory's call,
" From your mild eyes the show'rs of sorrow fall ?—
" The light of Excellence, that round you glows,
" Decks with reflected beam your Brother's brows!
" Oh! may his Fame, in some distinguish'd day,
' Pour on that Excellence the brightest ray !

" Dim clouds of Woe! ye veil each sprightly grace
" That us'd to sparkle in MARIA's face.
" My *tuneful ANNA to her lute complains,
" But Grief's fond throbs arrest the parting strains.
" Fair as the silver blossom on the thorn,
" Soft as the spirit of the vernal morn,
" LOUISA, chace those trembling fears, that prove
" Th' ungovern'd terrors of a Sister's love.
" They bend thy sweet head, like yon lucid flow'r,
" That shrinks and fades beneath the summer's show'r.

* *Tuneful Anna.*—Miss Anne Andre has a poetical talent.

Y

" Oh ! smile, my Sisters, on this destin'd day,

" And with the radiant omen gild my way !

" And thou, my Brother, gentle as the gale,

" Whose breath perfumes anew the blossom'd vale,

" Yet quick of spirit, as th' electric beam,

" When from the clouds its darting lightnings stream,

" Soothe with incessant care our Mother's woes,

" And hush her anxious sighs to soft repose.

" And be ye sure, when distant far I stray

" To share the dangers of the arduous day,

" Your tender faithful amity shall rest

" The * last dear record of my grateful breast.

" Oh ! graceful Priestess at the fane of Truth,

" Friend of my soul ! and guardian of my youth !

" Skill'd to convert the duty to the choice,

" My gentle Mother !---in whose melting voice

" The virtuous precept, that perpetual flow'd,

" With Music warbled, and with Beauty glow'd,

" Thy tears !---ah Heav'n ! not drops of molten lead,

" Pour'd on thy hapless Son's devoted head,

* *Last dear record.*—" I have a Mother, and three Sisters, to
" whom the value of my commission wou'd be an object, as the
" loss of Grenada has much affected their income. It is need-
" less to be more explicit on this subject, I know your Excel-
" lency's goodness."——See Major Andre's last letter to General
Clinton, published in the Gazette.

" With keener smart had each sensation torn !

" They wake the nerve where agonies are born !

" But oh! restrain me not !---thy tender strife,

" What wou'd it save?---alas! thy ANDRE's life !

" Oh! what a weary pilgrimage 'twill prove

" Strew'd with the thorns of disappointed love !

" Ne'er can he break the charm, whose fond controul,

" By habit rooted, lords it o'er his soul,

" If here he languish in inglorious ease,

" Where Science palls, and Pleasures cease to please.

" 'Tis Glory only, with her potent ray,

" Can chace the clouds that darken all his way.

" Then dry those pearly drops that wildly flow,

" Nor snatch the laurel from my youthful brow !

" The Rebel-Standard blazes to the noon !

" And Glory's path is bright before thy Son !

" Then join thy voice! and thou with Heav'n ordain

" While ANDRE lives, he may not live in vain ! "

He says !---and sighing seeks the busy strand,

Where anchor'd Navies wait the wish'd command.

To the full gale the nearer billows roar,

And proudly lash the circumscribing shore ;

While furious on the craggy coast they rave,

All calm and lovely rolls the distant wave ;

For onward, as th' unbounded waters spread,
Deep sink the rocks in their capacious bed,
And all their pointed terrors utmost force,
But gently interrupts the billows' course.

So on his present hour rude Passion preys!
So smooth the prospect of his future days!
Unconscious of the storm, that grimly sleeps,
To wreck its fury on th' unshelter'd deeps!

Now yielding waves divide before the prow,
The white sails bend, the streaming pennants glow;
And swiftly waft him to the western plain,
Where fierce Bellona rages o'er the slain.

Firm in their strength opposing legions stand,
Prepar'd to drench with blood the thirsty land.
Now Carnage hurls her flaming bolts afar,
And Desolation groans amid the war.
As bleed the valiant, and the mighty yield,
Death stalks, the only victor o'er the field.

Foremost in all the horrors of the day,
Impetuous * ANDRE leads the glorious way;

* *Impetuous Andre.*—It is iu this passage only that fiction has
been employed through the narrative of the poem. Mr. Andre

Till, rashly bold, by numbers forc'd to yield,
They drag him captive from the long-fought field.
Around the Hero croud th' exulting bands,
And seize the spoils of war with bloody hands;
Snatch the dark plumage from his awful crest,
And tear the golden crescent from his breast;
The sword, the tube, that wings the death from far,
And all the fatal implements of war!

Silent, unmov'd the gallant Youth survey'd
The lavish spoils triumphant ruffians made.
The idle ornament, the useless spear,
He little recks, but oh! there is a fear
Pants with quick throb, while yearning sorrows dart
Thro' his chill frame, and tremble at his heart.

" What tho' HONORA's voice no more shall charm!
" No more her beamy smile my bosom warm!
" Yet from these eyes shall force for ever tear
" The sacred Image of that form so dear?---
" Shade * of my Love! tho' mute and cold thy charms,
Ne'er hast thou blest my happy rival's arms!

was a prisoner in America, soon after his arrival there, but the
author is unacquainted with the circumstances of the action in
which he was taken.

* *Shade of my Love.*—The miniature of Honora. A letter

" To my sad heart each dawn has seen thee prest !

" Each night has laid thee pillow'd on my breast !

" Force shall not tear thee from thy faithful shrine;

" Shade of my Love ! thou shalt be ever mine !

" 'Tis fix'd !---these lips shall resolute inclose

" The precious soother of my ceaseless woes.

" And shou'd relentless Violence invade

" This last retreat, by frantic fondness made,

" One way remains !---Fate whispers to my soul

" Intrepid * Portia and her burning coal !

" So shall the throbbing inmate of my breast

" From Love's sole gift meet everlasting rest ! "

While these sad thoughts in swift succession fire

The smother'd embers of each fond desire,

from Major Andre to one of his friends, written a few years ago,
contained the following sentence. " I have been taken prisoner
" by the Americans, and stript of every thing except the picture
" of Honora, which I concealed in my mouth. Preserving
" that, I yet think myself fortunate."

* *Intrepid Portia.*]—" BRUTUS. Impatient of my absence,
" And grieved that young Octavius, with Mark Anthony
" Had made themselves so strong, she grew distracted.
" And, her Attendants absent, swallow'd fire.
" CASSIUS.] And dy'd so ?
" BRUTUS.] Even so !

See Shakspeare's Play of Julius Cæsar, Act IV. Sc. IV.

Quick to his mouth his eager hand removes
The beauteous semblance of the form he loves.
That darling treasure safe, resign'd he wears
The sordid robe, the scanty viand shares;
With chearful fortitude content to wait
The barter'd ransom of a kinder fate.

Now many a Moon in her pale course had shed
The pensive beam on ANDRE's captive head.
At length the Sun rose jocund, to adorn
With all his splendor the enfranchis'd morn.
Again the Hero joins the ardent train
That pours its thousands on the tented plain;
And shines distinguish'd in the long array,
Bright as the silver star that leads the day!
His modest temperance, his wakeful heed,
His silent diligence, his ardent speed,
Each warrior-duty to the veteran taught,
Shaming the vain experience time had brought.
Dependence scarcely feels his gentle sway,
He shares each want, and smiles each grief away?
And to the virtues of a noble heart,
Unites the talents of inventive art.
Thus from his swift and faithful pencil flow
The Lines, the Camp, the Fortress of the Foe:

Serene to counteract each deep design,
Points the dark ambush, and the springing mine;
Till, as a breathing incense, ANDRE's name
Pervades the host, and swells the loud acclaim.

The CHIEF no virtue views with cold regard,
Skill'd to discern, and generous to reward ;
Each tow'ring hope his honor'd smiles impart,
As near his person, and more near his heart
The graceful Youth he draws,---and round his brow
Bids Rank and Pow'r their mingled brilliance throw.

Oh! hast thou seen a blooming morn of May
In crystal beauty shed the modest ray,
And with its balmy dew's refreshing show'r
Swell the young grain, and ope the purple flow'r,
In bright'ning lustre reach its radiant noon,
Rob'd in the gayest mantle of the Sun ?
Then 'mid the splendors of its azure skies,
Oh! hast thou seen the cruel storm arise,
In sable horror shroud each dazzling charm,
And dash their glories back with icy arm ?

Thus lowr'd the deathful cloud amid the blaze
Of ANDRE's rising hopes,---and quench'd their rays !

Ah fatal Embassy !---thy hazards dire
His kindling soul with ev'ry ardor fire ;
Great CLINTON gives it to the courage prov'd,
And the known wisdom of the friend he lov'd.

As fair Euryalus, to meet his fate,
With Nysus rushes from the Dardan gate,
Relentless Fate ! whose fury scorns to spare
The snowy breast, red lip, and shining hair,
So polish'd ANDRE launches on the waves,
Where * Hudson's tide its dreary confine laves.
With firm intrepid foot the youth explores
Each dangerous pathway of the hostile shores ;
But on no Veteran-Chief his step attends,
As silent round the gloomy wood he wends ;
Alone he meets the brave repentant foe,
Sustains his late resolve, receives his vow,
With ardent skill directs the doubtful course,
Seals the firm bond, and ratifies its force.

'Tis thus AMERICA, thy Generals fly,
And wave new banners in their native sky !

* *Hudson's tide.*—Major Andre came up the Hudson river to
meet General Arnold. On his return by land he fell into the
hands of the enemy.

Sick of the mischiefs artful GALLIA pours,
In friendly semblance on thy ravag'd shores.
Unnatural compact!---shall a race of slaves
Sustain the ponderous standard Freedom waves?
No! while their feign'd protection spreads the toils,
The Vultures hover o'er the destin'd spoils!
How fade Provincial-glories, while ye run
To court far deeper bondage than ye shun!
Is this the generous active rising flame,
That boasted Liberty's immortal name,
Blaz'd for its rights infring'd, its trophies torn,
And taught the Wise the dire mistake to mourn,
When haughty BRITAIN, in a luckless hour,
With rage iuebriate, and the lust of pow'r,
To fruitless conquest, and to countless graves
Led her gay Legions o'er the western waves?
The Fiend of Discord, cow'ring at the prow,
Sat darkly smiling at th' impending woe!

Long did my soul the wretched strife survey,
And wept the horrors of the deathful day;
Thro' rolling years saw undecisive War
Drag bleeding Wisdom at his iron car:
Exhaust my country's treasure, pour her gore
In fruitless conflict on the distant shore;

Saw the firm Congress all her might oppose,
And while I mourn'd her fate, rever'd her foes.

But when, repentant of her prouder aim,
She gently waves the long disputed claim ;
Extends the Charter with your Rights restor'd,
And hides in olive-wreaths the blood-stain'd sword ;
Then to reject her peaceful wreaths, and throw
Your Country's Freedom to our mutual Foe !---
Infatuate land ?---from that detested day
Distracted councils, and the thirst of sway,
Rapacious Avarice, Superstition vile,
And all the *Frenchman* dictates in his guile
Disgrace your Congress !---Justice drops her scale !
And radiant Liberty averts her sail !
They fly indignant the polluted plain,
Where Truth is scorn'd, and Mercy pleads in vain.

That she does plead in vain, thy witness bear,
Accursed hour ?---thou darkest of the year !
That with Misfortune's deadliest venom fraught,
To Tappan's wall the gallant Andre brought.

Oh Washington ! I thought thee great and good,
Nor knew thy Nero-thirst of guiltless blood !

Severe to use the pow'r that Fortune gave,

Thou cool determin'd Murderer of the Brave!

Lost to each fairer virtue, that inspires

The genuine fervor of the Patriot fires!

And You, the base Abettors of the doom,

That sunk his blooming honours in the tomb,

Th' opprobrious tomb your harden'd hearts decreed,

While all he ask'd was as the brave to bleed!

Nor other boon the glorious Youth implor'd,

Save the cold mercy of the warrior-sword!

O dark, and pitiless! your impious hate

O'er-whelm'd the Hero in the Ruffian's fate!

Stopt with the * Feloncord the rosy breath!

And venom'd with disgrace the darts of Death!

Remorseless WASHINGTON! the day shall come

Of deep repentance for this barb'rous doom!

When injur'd ANDRE's memory shall inspire

A kindling army with resistless fire;

* *Felon-cord.*—" As I suffer in the defence of my country, I must consider this hour as the most glorious of my life.—Remember that I die as becomes a British Officer, while the manner of my death must reflect disgrace on your Commander."

See Major Andre's last words, inserted in the General Evening Post, for Tuesday, November the 14th, 1780.

Each falchion sharpen that the Britons wield,
And lead their fiercest Lion to the field !
Then, when each hope of thine shall set in night,
When dubious dread, and unavailing flight
Impel your host, thy guilt-upbraided soul
Shall wish untouch'd the sacred life you stole !
And when thy heart appall'd, and vanquish'd pride
Shall vainly ask the mercy they deny'd,
With horror shalt thou meet the fate they gave,
Nor Pity gild the darkness of thy grave !
For Infamy, with livid hand shall shed
Eternal mildew on the ruthless head !

Less cruel far than thou, on Ilium's plain,
Achilles, raging for Patroclus slain !
When hapless Priam bends the aged knee,
To deprecate the victor's dire decree,
The nobler Greek, in melting pity spares
The lifeless Hector to his Father's pray'rs,
Fierce as he was ;---'tis *Cowards* only know
Persisting vengeance o'er a *fallen* foe.

But no intreaty wakes the soft remorse,
Oh murdered ANDRE ! for thy sacred corse ;
Vain were an army's, vain its Leader's sighs !---
Damp in the earth on Hudson's shore it lies !

Unshrouded welters in the wint'ry storm,
And gluts the riot of the * Tappan worm!
But Oh! its dust, like Abel's blood, shall rise,
And call for justice from the angry skies!

What tho' the Tyrants, with malignant pride,
To thy pale corse each decent rite deny'd!
Thy graceful limbs in no kind covert laid,
Nor with the Christian-Requiem sooth'd thy shade!
Yet on thy grass-green bier soft April-show'rs
Shall earliest wake the sweet spontaneous flow'rs!
Bid the blue hare-bell, and the snow-drop there
Hang their cold cup, and drop the pearly tear!
And oft, at pensive Eve's ambiguous gloom,
Imperial Honour, bending o'er thy tomb,
With solemn strains shall lull thy deep repose,
And with his deathless laurels shade thy brows!

Lamented Youth! while with inverted spear
The British legions pour th' indignant tear!
Round the dropt arm the * funeral-scarf entwine,
And in their hearts' deep core thy worth enshrine;

---

* *Tappan.* —The place where Major Andre was executed.

Funeral-scarf.—Our whole army in America went into mourning for Major Andre, a distinguished tribute to his merit.

While my weak Muse, in fond attempt and vain,

But feebly pours a perishable strain,

Oh! ye distinguish'd few! whose glowing lays

Bright Phœbus kindles with his purest rays,

Snatch from its radiant source the living fire,

And light with * Vestal flame your ANDRE'S HAL-
      LOWED PYRE!

* *Vestal flame.*—The Vestal fire was kept perpetually burning, and originally kindled from the rays of the sun.

LETTERS

ADDRESSED TO

THE AUTHOR OF THE FOREGOING POEM,

BY

MAJOR ANDRE,

WHEN HE WAS A YOUTH OF EIGHTEEN.

LETTER I.

Clapton, Oct. 3, 1769.

FROM their agreeable excursion to Shrewsbury, my
dearest friends are by this time returned to their
thrice beloved Lichfield ; once again have they beheld
those fortunate *spires*, the constant witnesses of all
their pains and pleasures.   I can well conceive the
emotions of joy which their first appearance, from the
neighbouring hills, excites after absence ; they seem
to welcome you home, and invite you to reiterate those
hours of happiness, of which they are a species of
monument.   I shall have an eternal love and reverence for them.   Never shall I forget the joy that
danced in Honora's eyes, when she first shewed them
to me from Needwood Forest on our return with you
from Buxton to Lichfield.   I remember she called
them the *ladies of the valley*——their lightness
and elegance deserve the title.   Oh! how I loved
them from that instant !   My enthusiasm concerning

z 2

them is carried farther even than your's and Honora's, for every object that has a pyramidal form, recals them to my recollection, with a sensation, that brings the tear of pleasure into my eyes.

How happy must you have been at Shrewsbury? only that you tell me, alas! that dear Honora was not so well as you wished during your stay there.—I always hope the best. My impatient spirit rejects every obtruding idea, which I have not fortitude to support. Doctor Darwin's skill, and your tender care will remove that sad pain in her side, which makes writing troublesome and injurious to her; which robs her poor * Cher Jean of those precious pages, with which, he flatters himself, she would otherwise have indulged him,

So your happiness at Shrewsbury scorned to be indebted to public amusements---Five Virgins---united in the soft bonds of friendship! How I should have liked to have made the sixth! But you surprize me by such an absolute exclusion of the Beaux; I certainly thought that when five wise virgins were watch-

* A name of kindness, by which Mr. Andre was often called by his mother and sisters, and generally adopted by the persons mentioned in these letters,

ing at midnight, it must have been in expectation of
the bridegroom's coming. *We* are at this instant five
virgins, writing round the same table---my three sisters, Mr. Ewer, and myself. I beg no reflections
injurious to the honour of poor *Cher Jean.* My mother is gone to pay a visit, and has left us in possession
of the old coach; but as for nags, we can boast of
only two long-tails, and my sisters say they are sorry
cattle, being no other than my friend Ewer and myself, who, to say truth, have enormous pig-tails.

My dear Boissier is come to town; he has brought
a little of the soldier with him, but he is the same
honest, warm, intelligent friend I always found him.
He sacrifices the town diversions, since I will not par-
take of them.

We are jealous of your correspondents, who are so
numerous. Yet, write to the Andres often, my dear
Julia, for who are they that will value your letters
quite so much as we value them ?---The least scrap of
a letter will be received with the greatest joy; write
therefore, tho' it were only to give us the comfort of
having a piece of paper which has recently passed
thro' your hands; Honora will put in a little postcript, were it only to tell me that she is *my very sin-*

cere friend, who will neither give me love nor comfort---very short indeed, Honora, was thy last postcript!——But I am too presumptuous; I will not scratch out, but I *un*say ; from the little there *was* I received more joy than I deserve.—This *Cher Jean* is an impertinent fellow, but he will grow discreet in time; you must consider him as a poor novice of *eighteen*, who, for all the sins he may commit, is sufficiently punished in the single evil of being 120 miles from Lichfield.

My mother and sisters will go to Putney in a few days to stay some time ; we none of us like Clapton ; *I* need not care, for I am all day long in town; but it is avoiding Scylla to fall into Charybdis. You paint to me the pleasant vale of Stow in the richest autumnal colouring : in return I must tell you, that my zephyrs are wafted through cracks in the wainscot ; for murmuring streams I have dirty kennels ; for bleating flocks, grunting pigs ; and squalling cats for birds that incessantly warble ; I have said something of this sort in my letter to Miss Spearman, and am twinged with the idea of these epistles being confronted, and that I shall recal to your memory the fat Knight's love letters to Mrs. Ford and Mrs. Page.

Julia, perhaps thou fanciest I am merry—Alas!—
But I do not wish to make you as doleful as myself;
and besides, when I would express the tender feelings
of my soul, I have no language which does them any
justice; if I had, I should regret that you could not
have it fresher, and that whatever one communicates
by letter must go such a round-about way, before it,
reaches one's correspondent; from the writer's heart
thro' his head, arm, hand, pen, ink, paper, over
many a weary hill and dale, to the eye, head, and
heart of the reader. I have often regretted our not
possessing a sort of faculty which should enable our
sensations, remarks, &c. to arise from their source in
a sort of exhalation, and fall upon our paper in words
and phrases properly adapted to express them, without passing through an imagination whose operations
so often fail to second those of the heart. Then what
a metamorphose should we see in people's stile! How
eloquent those who are truly attached! how stupid
they who falsely profess affection! Perhaps the
former had never been able to express half their regard; while the latter, by their flowers of rhetoric,
had made us believe a thousand times more than they
ever felt---but this is whimsical moralizing.

My sisters Penserosos were dispersed on their arrival in town, by the joy of seeing Louisa and their dear little brother Billy again, our kind and excellent uncle Giradot, and uncle Lewis Andre. I was glad to see them, but they complained, not without reason, of the gloom upon my countenance---Billy wept for joy that we were returned, while poor *Cher Jean* was ready to weep for sorrow. Louisa is grown still handsomer since we left her. Our sisters, Mary and Anne, knowing your partiality to beauty, are afraid that when they shall introduce her to you, she will put their noses out of joint. Billy is not old enough for me to be afraid of in the rival-way, else I should keep him aloof, for his heart is formed of those affectionate materials, so dear to the ingenuous taste of Julia and her Honora.

I sympathize in your resentment against the canonical Dons, who stumpify the heads of those good green * people, beneath whose friendly shade so many of your happiest hours have glided away: but they defy them : let them stumpify as much as they please, time will repair the mischief---their verdant arms will again extend, and invite you to their shelter.

The evenings grow long ; I hope your conversation

* The trees in the Cathedral walk in Lichfield.

round the fire will sometimes fall on the Andres; it will be a great comfort that they are remembered. We chink our glasses to your healths at every meal; here's to our Lichfieldian friends, says Nanny;--- Oh---h, says Mary;---with all my soul, say I;--- Allons, cries my mother;---and the draught seems nectar. The libation made, we begin our uncloying theme, and so beguile the gloomy evening.

Mr. and Mrs. Seward will accept my most affectionate respects. My male friend at Lichfield will join in your conversation on the Andres. Among the numerous good qualities he is possessed of, he certainly has gratitude, and then he cannot forget those who so sincerely love and esteem him; I, in particular, shall always recall with pleasure the happy hours I have passed in his company; my friendship for him, and for your family, has diffused itself, like the precious ointment from Aaron's beard, on every thing which surrounds you, therefore I beg you would give my amitiès to the whole town. Persuade Honora to forgive the length and ardor of the inclosed, and believe me truly

your affectionate and faithful friend,

J. ANDRE.

LETTER II.

———

London, October 19, 1769.

FROM the midst of books, papers, bills, and other implements of gain, let me lift up my drowsy head a while to converse with dear Julia. And first, as I know she has a fervent wish to see me a quill-driver, I must tell her, that I begin, as people are wont to do, to look upon my future profession with great partiality. I no longer see it in so disadvantageous a light. Instead of figuring a merchant as a middle-aged man, with a bob wig, a rough beard, in snuff coloured clothes, grasping a guinea in his red hand; I conceive a comely young man, with a tolerable pig-tail, wielding a pen with all the noble fierceness of the Duke of Marlborough brandishing a truncheon upon a sign-post, surrounded with types and emblems, and canopied with cornucopiæs that disembogue their stores upon his head; Mercuries reclin'd upon bales of goods; Genii playing with pens, ink, and paper;

while in perspective, his gorgeous vessels " launched on the bosom of the silver Thames," are wafting to distant lands the produce of this commercial nation. Thus all the mercantile glories croud on my fancy, emblazoned in the most refulgent colouring of an ardent imagination; borne on her soaring pinions I wing my flight to the time when Heaven shall have crowned my labours with success and opulence. I see sumptuous palaces rising to receive me; I see orphans, and widows, and painters, and fidlers, and poets, and builders, protected and encouraged; and when the fabrick is pretty nearly finished by my shattered Pericranium, I cast my eyes around, and find John Andre, by a small coal fire, in a gloomy comptinghouse in Warnford Court, nothing so little as what he has been making himself, and in all probability never to be much more than he is at present. But oh! my dear Honora!---it is for thy sake only I wish for wealth. You say she was somewhat better at the time you wrote last. I must flatter myself that she will soon be without any remains of this threatening disease.

It is seven o'clock---You and Honora, with two or three more select friends, are now probably encircling your dressing-room fire-place. What would I not give to enlarge that circle ! The idea of a clean hearth, and a snug circle round it, formed by a few sincere friends, transports me. You seem combined together against the inclemency of the weather, the hurry, bustle, ceremony, censoriousness, and envy of the world. The purity, the warmth, the kindly influence of fire, to all for whom it is kindled, is a good emblem of the friendship óf such amiable minds as Julia's and her Honora's. Since I cannot be there in reality, pray imagine me with you; admit me to your conversationès; think how I wish for the blessing of joining them! and be persuaded that I take part in all your pleasures, in the dear hope, that e'er it be very long, your blazing hearth will burn again for me. Pray keep me a place; let the poker, tongs, or shovel, represent me: but you have Dutch-tiles, which are infinitely better; so let Moses, or Aaron, or Balaam's ass be my representative.

But time calls me to Clapton. I quit you abruptly till to-morrow: when, if I do not tear the nonsense I have been writing, I may perhaps increase its quantity. Signora Cynthia is in clouded majesty. Silvered with her beams I am about to jog to Clapton upon my own stumps; musing as I homeward plod my way---Ah! need I name the subject of my contemplations?

Thursday.

I had a sweet walk home last night, and found the Claptonians, with their fair guest, a Miss Mourgue, very well. My sisters send their amitiès, and will write in a few days.

This morning I returned to town; it has been the finest day imaginable; a solemn mildness was diffused throughout the blue horizon; its light was clear and distinct rather than dazzling; the serene beams of the autumnal sun!---Gilded hills, variegated woods, glittering spires, ruminating herds, bounding flocks, all combined to inchant the eyes, expand the heart, and " chace all sorrow but despair."---In the midst of such a scene, no lesser grief can prevent our sympathy with nature; a calmness, a benevolent disposition seizes us with sweet insinuating power. The very brute creation seem sensible of these beauties; there is a species of mild cheerfulness in the face of a lamb, which I have but indifferently expressed in a corner of my paper, and a demure contented look in an ox,

which, in the fear of expressing still worse, I leave
unattempted.

Business calls me away; I must dispatch my letter;
yet what does it contain ?---No matter; you like any
thing better than news. Indeed you never told me
so, but I have an intuitive knowledge upon the subject, from the sympathy which I have constantly perceived in the taste of Julia and Cher Jean. What is
it to you or me

> If here in the city we have nothing but riot,
> If the Spital-field Weavers can't be kept quiet,
> If the weather is fine, or the streets should be dirty,
> Or if Mr. Dick Wilson died aged of thirty?

—But if I was to hearken to the versifying grumbling
I feel within me I should fill my paper, and not have
room left to intreat that you would plead my cause to
Honora more eloquently than the inclosed letter has
the power of doing. Apropos of verses, you desire
me to recollect my random description of the engaging appearance of the charming Mrs.——. Here
it is at your service:

> Then rustling and bustling the Lady comes down,
> With a flaming red face, and a broad yellow gown,
> And a hobbling out-of-breath gait, and a frown.

This little French cousin of ours, Delarise, was my

sister Mary's play-fellow at Paris. His sprightliness engages my sisters extremely. Doubtless they talk much of him to you in their letters.

How sorry I am to bid you adieu! Oh let me not be forgot by the friends most dear to you at Lichfield! *Lichfield!* Ah! of what magic letters is that little word composed! How graceful it looks when it is written! Let nobody talk to me of its original meaning---" * The field of blood!" Oh! no such thing! It is the field of joy! "The beautiful city, that lifts her fair head in the valley and says, I *am*, and there is none beside me!" Who says she is vain? Julia will not say so, nor yet Honora, and least of all their devoted

J. ANDRE.

* *Field of blood.*—Here is a small mistake—Lichfield is not the field of blood, but "the field of dead bodies," alluding to a battle fought between the Romans and the British Christians in the Dioclesian persecution, when the latter were massacred. Three slain kings, with their burying-place, now Barrowcophill, and the Cathedral in miniature, form the city-arms. *Lich* is still a word in use. The church-yard gates, through which funerals pass, are often called Lich-gates, vulgarly Light-gates.

LETTER III.

———

Clapton, November 1, 1769.

My ears still ring with the sounds of Oh Jack! Oh Jack! How do the dear Lichfieldians?---What do they say?---What are they about?---What did *you* do while you were with them?---Have patience, said I, good people! and began my story, which they devoured with as much joyful avidity as Adam did Gabriel's tidings of Heaven. My mother and sisters are all very well, and delighted with their little Frenchman, who is a very agreeable lad.

Surely you applaud the fortitude with which I left you! Did I not come off with flying colours? It was a great effort, for, alas! this recreant heart did *not second* the smiling courage of the *countenance;* nor is it yet as it ought to be, from the hopes it may reasonably entertain of seeing you all again e'er the winter's dreary hours are past. Julia, my dear Julia, gild them with tidings of our beloved Honora! Oh that you may be enabled to tell me that she regains her health, and her charming vivacity! Your sympathizing heart partakes all the joys and pains of your friends. Never can I forget its kind offices, which were of such moment to my peace! *Mine* is formed for friendship, and I am blest in being able to place so *well* the purest passion of an ingenuous mind! How am I honoured in Mr. and Mrs. Seward's attachment to me! Charming were the anticipations which beguiled the long tracts of hill, and dale, and plain, that divide London from Lichfield! With what delight my eager eyes *drank* their first view of the dear spires! What rapture did I not feel on entering your gates! in flying up the hall steps! in rushing into the dining-room! in meeting the gladden'd eyes of dear Julia and her enchanting friend! That instant convinced me of the truth of Rousseau's observation, " that there are *moments* worth ages." Shall not those moments return? Ah Julia! the cold hand of absence is heavy upon the heart of your poor *Cher Jean !* He is forced to hammer into it perpetually every consoling argument that the magic wand of Hope can conjure up; viz. that every moment of industrious absence advances his journey, you know whither. I may sometimes make excursions to Lichfield, and

bask in the light of my Honora's eyes ! Sustain me
Hope ! nothing on my part shall be wanting which
may induce thee to *fulfil* thy blossoming promises.

The happy social circle, Julia, Honora, Miss
S——n, Miss B——n, her brother, Mr. S——e,
Mr. R——— n, &c. &c. are now, perhaps, enlivening
your dressing-room, the dear *blue region*, as Honora
calls it, with the sensible observation, the tasteful
criticism, or the elegant song ; dreading the iron-
tongue of the nine o'clock bell, which disperses the
beings, whom friendship and kindred virtues had
drawn together. My imagination attaches itself to
all, even the *inanimate* objects which surround Honora
and her Julia ; that have beheld their graces and virtues expand and ripen ; my dear Honora's, from
their infant bud.

The sleepy Claptonian train are gone to bed, somewhat wearied with their excursion to Enfield, whither
they have this day carried their favourite little Frenchman ; so *great* a favourite, the parting was quite tragical. I walked hither from town, as usual, to night ;
no hour of the twenty-four is so precious to me as that
devoted to this solitary walk. Oh, my friend ! I am
far from possessing the patient frame of mind which I

so continually invoke! Why is Lichfield an hundred and twenty miles from me? There is no *moderation* in the distance! Fifty or sixty miles had been a great deal too much, but *then*, there would have been less opposition from *authority* to my frequent visits; I conjure you, supply the want of these blessings by frequent *letters;* I must not, will not ask them of Honora, since the use of the pen is forbid to her declining health; I will content myself, as usual, with a postscript from her in your epistles. My sisters are charmed with the packet which arrived yesterday, and which they will answer soon.

As yet I have said nothing of our journey. We met an entertaining Irish Gentleman at Dunchurch, and, being fellow-sufferers in cold and hunger, joined interests, ordered four horses, and stuffed three in a chaise. It is not to *you*, I need apologize for talking in raptures of an Higler, whom we met on our road. His cart had passed us, and was at a considerable distance, when, looking back, he perceived that our chaise had stopped, and that the driver seemed mending something. He ran up to him, and with a face full of honest anxiety, pity, good-nature, and every sweet affection under Heaven, asked him if he wanted any thing? that he had plenty of nails, ropes, &c.

in his cart. That wretch of a postillion made no other reply than, " We want nothing Master." From the same impulse the good Irishman, Mr. Till, and myself, thrust our heads instantly out of the chaise, and tried to recompense to the honest creature this surly reply, by every kind and grateful acknowledgment, and by forcing upon him a little pecuniary tribute. My benevolence will be the warmer, while I live, for the treasured remembrance of this Higler's countenance.

I know you interest yourself in my destiny : I have now completely subdued my aversion to the profession of a merchant, and hope in time to acquire an inclination for it. Yet, God forbid I should ever love what I am to make the object of my attention ! that vile trash, which I care not for, but only as it may be the future means of procuring the blessing of my soul. Thus all my mercantile calculations go to the tune of *dear Honora.* When an impertinent consciousness whispers in my ear, that I am not of the right stuff for a merchant, I draw my Honora's picture from my bosom, and the sight of that dear Talisman so inspirits my industry, that no toil appears oppressive.

The poetic task you set me is in a sad method; my head and heart are too full of other matters to be engrossed by a draggle-tail'd wench of the Heliconian puddle.

I am going to try my interest in parliament; how you stare! it is to procure a frank. Be so good to give the inclosed to Honora; *it* will speak to *her;* and do *you* say every thing that is kind for me to every *other* distinguished friend of the dressing-room circle; encourage them in their obliging desire of scribbling in your letters, but don't let them take Honora's corner of the sheet.

Adieu!---May you all possess that cheerfulness denied to your *Cher Jean.* I fear it hurts my mother to see my musing moods; but I can neither help nor overcome them. The near hopes of another excursion to Lichfield, could alone disperse every gloomy vapour of my imagination.

Again, and yet again adieu!

J. ANDRE.

FINIS.

Printed by W. Clowes, Northumberland Court, Strand.

TO THE BINDER.

Portrait of Andre to face the title-page,

Map of North America to face page 1 of the Narrative.

Monument of Major Andre to face page 176.

———